KINGDOM Multiplication

KINGDOM Multiplication

52 Devotions to Unlock Financial Breakthrough and Live Generously on Purpose

Ron Eivaz

Carpenter's Son Publishing

Kingdom Multiplication: 52 Devotions to Unlock Financial Breakthrough and Live Generously on Purpose

Published by Carpenter's Son Publishing, Franklin, Tennessee

Cover and Interior Design by Suzanne Lawing

Printed in the United States of America

ISBN: 978-1-956370-99-7 (print)

ACKNOWLEDGEMENTS

Writing this book has been a process shaped by both real-life lessons and the input of key voices along the way.

To **Jennifer**, my wife—thank you for your strength, resilience, and commitment through the many seasons of ministry. Your presence and partnership have made a lasting impact on my life and calling.

To the **Harvest Church family**, thank you for being the proving ground for so much of what's written here. Thank you for being a living example of what generous, faith-filled, Kingdom-minded living looks like. Your hunger for God and willingness to step out in faith have inspired many of the stories and truths in these pages.

To **my team and staff**, who faithfully helped implement these teachings week by week—thank you for your diligence, feedback, and heart for excellence. This book grew out of what we built together.

To **Dave Williams** and **Phil Pringle**—before we became friends, you were mentors from a distance. Your teaching and example shaped how I understand generosity, Kingdom leadership, and what it means to build a church that truly makes an impact. I'm grateful for the clarity, conviction, and faith you've modeled—and for the influence you've had on my life and ministry.

And above all, to **Jesus Christ**, the One who supplies seed to the sower and builds His Church—may everything in these pages ultimately point back to You and serve Your purposes in the earth. May this book honor You and fuel Your Church to live with boldness, generosity, and eternal purpose.

— Ron

INTRODUCTION

The Privilege of Being God's Instruments of Blessing

It is one of the greatest honors of our lives to be used by God—to not only know Him, but also to be a part of what He is doing on the earth. And one of the clearest ways we partner with Him is through generosity. We were never meant to be reservoirs of blessing—we were created to be rivers. From the very beginning, God's design was to bless His people so that they could be a blessing to the nations.

In **Deuteronomy 8:18**, God makes a powerful and often overlooked statement: *"You shall remember the* LORD *your God, for it is He who gives you power to get wealth, that He may establish His covenant which He swore to your fathers, as it is this day."* This verse highlights divine purpose, not selfish prosperity. The ability to generate wealth is granted to us not for personal indulgence, but to ensure that His covenant is upheld globally. This book was written with that purpose in mind.

Over the years, I've watched believers with sincere hearts live beneath their calling—not because they lacked love for God, but because they didn't understand the role of faith, obedience, and financial stewardship in the Kingdom. God's covenant includes healing, salvation, peace, and provision—but in order for us to walk in it and extend it to others, we must first experience it for ourselves. We can't give what we haven't received. And we can't overflow if we're spiritually and financially dry.

These 52 devotionals were not written from theory. They were written out of real life—week by week, line by line, as I taught our staff the principles of Kingdom giving, faith for provision, and multiplication. It wasn't just about raising offerings or funding ministry—it was about forming a mindset and a culture that aligns with God's Word. A culture where people don't just give occasionally or emotionally, but live generously and consistently, fueled by revelation.

You Were Meant to Multiply

From Genesis to Revelation, the heart of God is to bless and multiply. From the garden to the Great Commission, His mandate has remained the same: *"Be fruitful and multiply ... make disciples of all nations."*

But in order to fulfill this divine calling, we need provision. Vision without provision becomes frustration. And that's why God doesn't just call us—He equips us. He gives us the power to get wealth, not to build personal empires, but to extend His eternal Kingdom.

The local church is meant to be a storehouse of both spiritual and natural blessing. We're meant to feed the hungry, support missions, plant churches, reach cities, disciple leaders, and transform culture. But we can't do that without resources. And resources don't flow where there's fear, shame, or confusion about finances; they flow where there's faith.

That's why this book matters.

The Power of Alignment

Many believers give, but they don't always give with understanding. They tithe, they sow, they support the church—but something still feels stuck. The windows of heaven feel closed. They live in cycles of lack and limitation and wonder why they don't see the breakthrough the Bible promises.

In my experience, the issue is almost always *alignment*.

Deuteronomy 8 is a sobering reminder that it's possible to forget the Lord even while receiving from His hand. The Lord warned His people not to become proud or self-reliant when the blessing came. Why? Because the source of our provision is never our own strength—it is *God who gives power to get wealth.* When we forget that, we fall out of alignment. But when we remember it—when we honor God first—He honors us with supernatural increase.

These devotionals are designed to help bring your thinking and your habits back into alignment with God's Word. Each one is built on Scripture and filled with practical truths that will renew your mind, build your faith, and position you for greater blessing—not for your sake alone, but so that you can be a conduit of blessing to others.

Discipling a Culture of Generosity

If you're a pastor or ministry leader, let me speak directly to you for a moment: It is our responsibility to disciple people in every area of their walk with God—including their finances. Too often, we shy away from teaching on giving unless there's a budget crisis. But when we only teach out of urgency, we miss the opportunity to form a culture of cheerful, consistent, faith-filled generosity.

That's why the second chapter of this book is aimed at pastors—to give you a framework for how to use these weekly teachings to train your staff, volunteers, and leaders. You can read them aloud in a team meeting, send them out in a devotional email, or use them as inspiration for your own financial teachings. However you use them, let them serve as building blocks to create a culture where generosity is not an occasional act, it's a core identity.

Faith Comes by Hearing

F.F. Bosworth famously said, *"Faith begins where the will of God is known."* That's why this book is rooted in the Word. Week after week, the devotionals bring clarity about what God has said about giving, provision, blessing, and multiplication. As you read and teach these truths, faith will come. Mindsets will shift. And as people begin to understand why we give—and *what* we're giving into—their confidence will grow and the fruit will follow.

My heart in writing this book is simple: to see you and your church step fully into the provision of God, not just so your needs are met, but so that you become a powerful instrument of His covenant in the earth.

Let's Partner with Heaven

Now is the time for the Church to rise with strength and supernatural supply. The harvest is great. The world is in need. And the Kingdom must advance. But that won't happen through lack, fear, or small thinking. It will happen through a people who know their God, trust His Word, and step boldly into the power He gives to get wealth *so that His covenant might be established.*

You are not just a recipient of God's blessing—you are an agent of His blessing. Let this book be a tool that empowers you to live in that identity and disciple others to do the same.

Let's align with His heart, walk in His power, and release His provision—so that the world may know the goodness of our God.

CHAPTER 1

How to Use This Book for Personal Breakthrough

The Purpose of This Book

Let's be clear right from the start: this book is not just about money. It's about breakthrough.

God is not looking to just improve your financial situation—He wants to transform your mindset, increase your faith, and set you free from the limitations that have held you back for years. Financial increase is part of it, but the real goal is alignment with the principles of God's Kingdom.

The truth is, many believers are stuck financially, not because of lack of effort, but because of wrong beliefs. They work hard. They tithe. They try to save. But something still feels stuck. The ceiling won't break. The overflow never comes. Why?

Because giving is not primarily a financial issue—it's a **faith** issue.

When you give, you're not just moving money—you're making a statement: "I trust God more than I trust this." Giving becomes a spiritual act, a declaration of who your Source really is. That's why breakthrough rarely comes until the mindset shifts.

Why This Book Matters

If you've been living in survival mode, paycheck to paycheck, or under constant financial stress, this book is for you. If you've tithed but never really seen abundance, this book is for you. If you've ever wrestled with guilt over wanting more or feared what others would think if you prospered—this is for you.

This book is here to help you:

- tear down the lies that have kept you in lack,
- replace them with truth from God's Word,
- step into the bold, abundant life God designed for you to live.

Not for selfish gain—but so that you can fulfill your calling, support the gospel, bless others, and live free from fear about money.

Let's be honest: The Church has often avoided this topic out of fear of being misunderstood. Some have misused the message of prosperity, twisting it into manipulation or greed. But the danger of abuse doesn't cancel out the truth.

The Bible has a lot to say about money, provision, and blessing. And ignoring those parts doesn't make us more spiritual—it just keeps us in lack.

God is calling His people into alignment—into obedience, generosity, and supernatural increase—not so they can hoard wealth, but so they can change the world.

Faith, Not Formula

This book won't give you a three-step formula to wealth. God is not a vending machine. But He is a Father—and like any good Father, He wants to see His children thriving, not barely scraping by.

He wants you to have more than enough so you can:

- fund the vision He's given you,
- respond to needs around you,
- step out in faith without financial fear,
- show the world what it looks like to be under the blessing of God.

Throughout this book, you'll be challenged to rethink your beliefs, stretch your faith, and obey what God says—especially when it doesn't make natural sense. That's the path to breakthrough.

But none of it will matter if you just read these pages casually. So before you go further, stop and ask God for this:

"Lord, open my heart. Renew my mind. Let Your Word transform how I think about money, giving, and increase. I don't want to just learn—I want to live in breakthrough. In Jesus's name, amen."

A Note on Expectation

What you get from this book depends on how you approach it. If you read it hoping for tips and tricks, you might pick up a few things. But if you read it with expectation—hungry for transformation—you'll see breakthrough.

Why? Because God responds to faith.

Jesus never said, "Let it be done according to your hard work." He said, **"Let it be done to you according to your faith."** That applies to healing. It applies to relationships. And yes, it applies to finances too.

So as you move through each chapter, don't just read—lean in. Ask questions. Write things down. Pray over what hits your heart. And most of all, **expect God to move.**

Because He will.

God's Will for Your Financial Blessing

You'll never have faith for something you're not convinced is God's will.

Again, as F.F. Bosworth said, "Faith begins where the will of God is known." We can't have genuine faith for something if we don't know that it's God's will—and the only way to know His will is through His Word. That's why the devotionals in this book are grounded in Scripture: to reveal God's heart for generosity, provision, and blessing. As you read and meditate on the truths found in His Word, His will becomes clear—and as His will is made known, faith begins to rise. You won't be giving out of pressure or obligation, but out of a confident assurance that you are aligning with God's will and stepping into His promises.

That's why this section matters. Before you can believe God for increase, you have to be rooted in the truth that **God wants to bless you**—and that includes financially.

Not in a prosperity-gospel, name-it-claim-it kind of way. But in a biblical, purpose-driven, Kingdom-minded way. When your heart is right and your motives are Kingdom-aligned, **prosperity isn't a problem—it's a tool.**

Let's look at what the Word actually says.

"Beloved, I pray that you may prosper in all things and be in health, just as your soul prospers."

—3 John 2

"Let the LORD be magnified, who has pleasure in the prosperity of His servant."
— Psalm 35:27

These aren't prosperity slogans. These are scriptures. They reflect the heart of a Father who takes pleasure in seeing His children thrive—not struggle, not scrape by, not live in fear of bills.

The Lie of Holy Poverty

For years, many Christians have believed that poverty is somehow more spiritual. That lack is holy. That struggle makes you closer to God.

Where did that come from?

It's not in the Bible. Jesus never glorified poverty—He confronted it. He fed the hungry. He paid Peter's taxes supernaturally. He had a treasurer managing ministry finances. He multiplied food, brought in large catches of fish, and provided beyond expectation.

Lack was never the goal. And it shouldn't be yours either.

Some people confuse humility with lack. But being humble doesn't mean living in poverty—it means living in obedience. True humility says, "God, I'll do whatever You ask, and go wherever You send me." If that means living on little for a season, fine. If that means handling millions for the Kingdom, also fine.

The point is this: **Lack is not your permanent identity.**

Prosperity with a Purpose

This isn't about getting rich just to say you're blessed. God's blessing always comes with responsibility.

"You will be enriched in every way so that you can be generous on every occasion."
— 2 Corinthians 9:11 (NIV)

There it is—clear and simple. God enriches us so we can be generous. So we can send missionaries, fund outreaches, build churches, help the poor, and respond instantly when there's a need. When we have a revelation in our spirit concerning generosity, then there is a YES in our heart for opportunities to expand the Kingdom of God.

The world has enough self-serving wealth. What God is looking for are people He can trust with resources—people who will **use it to build, serve, and give.**

You're not called to chase money, but you are called to steward it. And when your heart is aligned with God's Kingdom, He can trust you with more.

Money Is a Tool—Not a Master

Some Christians avoid talking about finances because they've seen the abuse. They've seen people become obsessed with wealth or manipulative in how they teach giving.

Let's be clear: **Money is not evil.**

*"For the love of money is a root
of all kinds of evil."*
— 1 Timothy 6:10

It's the love of money—not money itself—that's the problem. When you love money, you serve it. When you serve God, money serves you.

Money is neutral. It takes on the character of whoever holds it. In the hands of a righteous person, it builds churches, rescues orphans, and feeds the poor. In the hands of the wicked, it becomes a weapon of destruction.

So stop fearing it. Stop avoiding it. Learn to master it. Use it as a tool to fulfill your assignment.

God's Pattern for Provision

In Scripture, God consistently blesses His people when they walk in faith, obedience, and generosity.

- **Abraham** obeyed God and became exceedingly wealthy—*"very rich in livestock, in silver, and in gold"* (Genesis 13:2).

- **Isaac** sowed during a famine and reaped a hundredfold in the same year (Genesis 26:12).

- **Joseph** operated in wisdom and ended up managing the wealth of a nation.

- **David** gave extravagantly to fund the temple—and left behind billions (in today's value).

- **Solomon** asked for wisdom, and God added wealth and honor as a bonus.

God hasn't changed.

He still responds to faith. He still honors obedience. He still multiplies what you place in His hands. The difference is, under the New Covenant, you don't have to qualify through performance—you simply walk in alignment with His will and operate by faith.

Settling the Issue in Your Heart

Before you go further in this book, you need to settle one thing once and for all: **God wants to bless me so I can be a blessing.**

Say it out loud.

Write it down.

Because until that truth sinks into your spirit, you'll resist the very provision God wants to give you. You'll feel guilty when opportunities come. You'll downplay God's goodness in your life. And you'll never experience the full freedom He intends.

But once you believe it—really believe it—your posture changes. You stop striving. You stop fearing lack. You stop apologizing for favor.

And you start walking like someone who knows: I'm blessed for a reason.

Breaking Financial Strongholds and Poverty Mindsets

One of the greatest barriers to financial breakthrough isn't external—it's internal. It's not inflation, not your job, not your background. It's how you think.

You can tithe faithfully and still live in lack if your mindset hasn't changed. Why? Because breakthrough begins in the mind. What you believe sets the ceiling for what you can receive.

What Is a Poverty Mindset?

A poverty mindset is more than just not having money. It's a way of thinking that expects lack, fears increase, and subconsciously rejects prosperity. It's a belief system, not a bank balance.

Here's what it sounds like:

- "I don't deserve to be blessed."
- "If I had more, I'd probably mess it up."
- "God will meet my needs, but I shouldn't expect more than that."
- "It's selfish to want abundance."
- "Money always causes problems."
- "I just need enough to get by."

These aren't just innocent thoughts—they are spiritual strongholds. And they keep people bound even when God is trying to pour out blessing.

"For the weapons of our warfare are not carnal but mighty in God for pulling down strongholds, casting down arguments and ... bringing every thought into captivity to the obedience of Christ."

— 2 Corinthians 10:4–5

A stronghold is a fortress in the mind—a pattern of thinking that resists truth. And when it comes to finances, many believers are stuck behind walls built by fear, guilt, and bad teaching.

The Roots of the Poverty Spirit

Where do these mindsets come from? A few common sources:

- **Religious tradition** that equates holiness with lack.
- **Family upbringing** where money was always tight, and struggle was normalized.
- **Shame** from past financial failures or debt.
- **Fear of judgment** from others who might accuse you of being materialistic.
- **Twisted theology** that taught more about sacrifice than stewardship.

If you've ever felt conflicted about wanting more, you're not alone. But that inner tug-of-war is not from God. He doesn't want you to be confused about His will for your life.

Jesus said:

*"The thief comes only to steal and kill
and destroy; I have come that they may have life,
and have it to the full."*
— John 10:10 (NIV)

A poverty mindset will steal your confidence, kill your dreams, and destroy your ability to give freely. It's time to take it down.

The Truth That Sets You Free

Let's replace those old thoughts with truth:

- God is not just a Provider—He's an Abundant Provider.
- You are not barely getting by—you are blessed and highly favored.
- You are not limited by your past—you are empowered by God's promises.
- You don't give to survive—you give from a place of overflow.

*"And God is able to bless you abundantly,
so that in all things at all times, having all that you need,
you will abound in every good work."*
— 2 Corinthians 9:8 (NIV)

This is the kind of mindset you need: abundance with purpose. You're not trying to build wealth to flaunt it—you're building so you can abound in every good work.

That's Kingdom thinking.

Do You Deserve to Be Blessed?

Let's tackle this directly: **Yes, you do.**

Not because you earned it. Not because you're perfect. But because you're a child of God. You're a co-heir with Christ. You've been made righteous by His blood, and every promise of God is *yes and amen* in Him.

Blessing is not a reward for performance—it's an inheritance for sons and daughters.

If the enemy can convince you that you're not worthy of increase, he doesn't have to steal your money—you'll block it yourself. You'll reject opportunities. You'll avoid promotion. You'll give less because you expect less.

But when you know who you are in Christ, your mindset shifts from "I hope God comes through" to "God *always* comes through."

Renewing Your Mind

Romans 12:2 gives the blueprint: **"Be transformed by the renewing of your mind."**

Transformation happens when you actively replace lies with truth. So here's how to renew your mind around money and provision:

1. **Expose the lie.** What belief are you carrying that's holding you back?
2. **Replace it with Scripture.** What does God's Word actually say about that area?
3. **Speak truth daily.** Your words shape your thinking. Declare truth until it becomes your instinct.
4. **Act in faith.** Every time you give, believe, or make a bold financial move, you're breaking strongholds.

It's not a one-time event. It's a process. But as you renew your mind, your reality begins to shift. Your faith grows. Your expectation rises. And blessing begins to flow—not just to you, but through you.

Reflection Questions

- What poverty mindsets have I believed, knowingly or unknowingly?
- How has my upbringing shaped my view of money?
- What scriptures can I meditate on to renew my thinking?
- Am I expecting "just enough," or am I believing for more than enough?

Take time with these. Write out your answers. Pray over them. Be honest with yourself and with God. This is the groundwork of breakthrough.

The Law of Sowing and Reaping

Everything in God's Kingdom operates by laws. Spiritual laws, just like natural ones, work whether you feel them or not. Gravity doesn't require your agreement to function—neither does sowing and reaping.

"As long as the earth endures, seedtime and harvest ... will never cease."
— Genesis 8:22 (NIV)

This is one of the most foundational laws in both the natural and spiritual world: **What you sow, you will reap.**

It applies to your words. Your time. Your attitude. Your relationships.

And yes—your finances.

Giving Is Planting, Not Losing

A poverty mindset sees giving as subtraction.

Kingdom thinking sees giving as sowing.

There's a huge difference. When a farmer puts seed in the ground, he doesn't mourn it. He doesn't think, *"There goes all my seed; what a waste."* He understands that buried seed isn't lost—it's multiplying.

When you give in faith, you're not taking a loss—you're starting a harvest.

"Whoever sows sparingly will also reap sparingly, and whoever sows generously will also reap generously."
— 2 Corinthians 9:6 (NIV)

The Bible doesn't say "whoever gives;"—it says "whoever sows." Why? Because giving in the Kingdom is never just donation—it's investment. You're sowing into spiritual soil, and the return is both supernatural and practical.

What Kind of Harvest Are You Expecting?

Too many believers give without expectation. They sow with no faith for a return, thinking it's more "humble" that way. But that's not how God set it up.

Every seed carries expectation. Farmers expect harvest. Investors expect return. And givers in the Kingdom should expect **God's increase.**

That's not greed—it's faith.

"Give, and it will be given to you. A good measure, pressed down, shaken together and running over, will be poured into your lap."
— Luke 6:38 (NIV)

If Jesus said *it will be given to you,* why would you expect anything less?

Types of Seeds—And Types of Soil

Let's be clear: Not all seed is money, and not all soil is equal.

You can sow:

- time
- encouragement
- resources
- mentorship
- forgiveness
- finances

And you can sow into:

- ministries
- people in need
- your local church
- Kingdom missions
- Spirit-led opportunities

But don't confuse random giving with Spirit-led sowing. The key to multiplication isn't just being generous—it's being **obedient.**

The most powerful seeds are the ones God tells you to sow—even when they stretch you.

The Power of Obedient Giving

Some of your biggest breakthroughs won't come from routine giving. They'll come from *faith-stretching, obedience-driven, gut-check moments* when God tells you to give more than makes sense.

Ask anyone who's lived this, and they'll tell you: The harvest is always bigger than the sacrifice.

Here's why—obedience triggers blessing. Always.

- Elijah told the widow at Zarephath to make him a meal first—and her supply never ran out (1 Kings 17).
- Isaac sowed during a famine—when it made no logical sense—and reaped a hundredfold (Genesis 26:12).
- The boy gave up his five loaves and two fish—and Jesus fed thousands with it (John 6).

What made their seed powerful? Obedience.

Don't give just to give. Don't give out of guilt. Give because God leads you—and then give with bold expectation.

God Multiplies Seeds, Not Intentions

God doesn't multiply what you think about giving. He multiplies what you actually give.

"Now he who supplies seed to the sower and bread for food will also supply and increase your store of seed and will enlarge the harvest of your righteousness."
— 2 Corinthians 9:10 (NIV)

He supplies the seed—but you still have to sow it.

Too many believers eat their seed. They use every bit of provision for survival or comfort, never planting any of it—and then wonder why there's no harvest.

You don't plant apples and expect oranges. You don't eat your seed and expect a harvest. You don't hold onto everything and then pray for abundance.

You sow. In faith. On purpose. And God multiplies.

What You Sow Comes Back Bigger

This is one of the most consistent truths in the Kingdom: What you give returns multiplied.

- Sow mercy, reap mercy.
- Sow encouragement, reap strength.
- Sow money, reap provision.
- Sow in tears, reap in joy.

The world teaches to hoard in tough times. God teaches to sow.

That's why giving in hard seasons carries so much power—it's not emotional, it's prophetic. You're declaring, "I trust the harvest more than I fear the drought."

And God responds to that kind of faith.

Reflection Questions

- Do I see giving as loss or planting?
- Have I been sowing sparingly—or generously?
- Am I giving out of routine or out of obedience?
- What kind of harvest am I believing God for?

Take time to answer these before moving on. Write them out. Ask the Holy Spirit to speak. You may find that the key to your next level isn't more hustle—it's a seed you've been holding on to.

How to Apply This Book for Personal Growth

Information doesn't change your life. **Revelation acted on does.**

You could read every page of this book, nod your head, highlight the powerful lines, and still walk away unchanged. Not because the principles don't work—but because they weren't applied.

God doesn't bless knowledge. He blesses **obedience.**

That's why this chapter is a call to action. Don't just read this book—work it. Treat it like a roadmap. Ask God to show you how to walk it out, one step at a time.

Here's how to make that shift from head knowledge to personal breakthrough.

1. Read With an Open Heart

The first step is mindset. If you go into this with skepticism or religious filters, you'll block what God is trying to say. The Word of God has the power to change your life—but only if you're willing to let it challenge you.

You might read things in this book that push against how you were raised or what you were taught about money. Don't just reject it—*wrestle with it.* Take it to Scripture. Pray about it. Ask the Holy Spirit to confirm what's true.

Be open. Be teachable. Growth starts there.

"He who has ears to hear, let him hear!"
— Matthew 11:15

Every time you sit down with a chapter, ask:
"God, what are You trying to teach me right now?"

2. Take Notes, Journal, and Reflect

Breakthrough doesn't usually happen in a flash. It happens when small truths sink deep and begin to reshape how you think, speak, and act.

Don't just underline. **Engage.**

- Write down what hits you.
- Journal what the Holy Spirit reveals.
- Track your journey.

There's something powerful about putting pen to paper—it helps seal revelation. It also becomes a record of your transformation. You'll look back months or years from now and see just how far God has brought you.

3. Pray Over Every Principle

This isn't just a book to be studied—it's one to be prayed through. Each time you come across a principle, take a moment and pray it into your life.

Example:

Principle: God is my Source.

Prayer: "Lord, I repent for trusting other sources more than You. I declare today that You are my Provider, and I will not fear lack. Teach me to trust You fully."

Make it personal. Make it real. Turn truth into conversation with God, and you'll find it gets planted deeper into your spirit.

4. Stretch Your Faith

Growth always involves a stretch.

If everything you read in this book feels safe or familiar, something's off. God will ask you to step into uncomfortable territory—not to punish you, but to grow your capacity for blessing.

He might ask you to give more than you've ever given.

He might challenge how you think about money, success, or provision.

He might stretch you to believe for things that seem way beyond your current circumstances.

Don't shrink back. Faith doesn't make sense—it moves mountains.

"Without faith it is impossible to please God."
— Hebrews 11:6 (NIV)

So stretch. Trust. And move.

5. Take Action, Even If It Doesn't Make Sense

One of the biggest themes of this book is simple but powerful: **Obey God. Period.**

Don't wait for perfect conditions.

Don't wait until you feel 100 percent ready.

Obey even when it doesn't make logical sense. Faith-filled obedience always precedes breakthrough.

"Trust in the Lord with all your heart and lean not on your own understanding."
— Proverbs 3:5

God may lead you to:

- forgive a debt someone owes you,
- sow a sacrificial seed,
- turn down a "safe" opportunity and step into something bigger,

- believe for a new stream of income when there's no sign of it yet.

Don't overthink it. Obey.

Every act of obedience opens the door to the supernatural.

6. Track the Results

This is crucial: **Write down what happens** as you apply these principles.

- unexpected checks in the mail
- debt forgiveness
- new business or job opportunities
- financial favor you didn't see coming
- ideas or strategies that bring increase
- peace and confidence in place of fear

Don't chalk it up to coincidence. Call it what it is—**God's faithfulness.**

Documenting your journey builds faith. When you feel discouraged or doubt creeps in, you'll have proof that God is working. And your testimony will not only strengthen you—it will inspire others.

7. Stay Committed

Breakthrough isn't always instant. Sometimes the harvest takes time. But if you stay consistent—sowing, obeying, trusting—you will see the fruit.

Don't let a delay become a discouragement.

God is not mocked. His principles don't fail. If He promised harvest, harvest is coming.

"Let us not become weary in doing good, for at the proper time we will reap a harvest if we do not give up."
— Galatians 6:9 (NIV)

Stay faithful. Stay generous. Stay expectant.

This is not a short-term message. It's a lifestyle shift.

The Power of Testimony and Expectation

If you're serious about walking in financial breakthrough, here's something you must do:

Track what God does—and talk about it.

Testimony is more than a nice story. It's spiritual warfare. It's proof that the Word works. And it builds faith for what's coming next.

"They overcame him by the blood of the Lamb and by the word of their testimony."
— Revelation 12:11

The enemy wants to keep you silent. He wants you to downplay miracles, hide your breakthroughs, and act like it's all coincidence. Why?

Because your testimony is contagious. When you share what God has done, faith multiplies. Others hear it and start believing for their own breakthrough.

It shifts atmospheres. It cracks open closed hearts. And it builds bold, expectant faith.

Write It Down—Every Win, Every Breakthrough

Don't just celebrate the big things. Capture everything:

- a bill paid off early
- a check in the mail you weren't expecting
- a new client or promotion
- divine strategy for your business
- peace replacing stress over finances
- doors opening without striving

Small breakthroughs are **seeds of bigger things.** If you'll steward them with gratitude and documentation, God will multiply them.

Keep a testimony journal. Put it in your phone if you have to. Review it often. It will anchor your faith when the enemy whispers, "Nothing's changing."

Expectation Sets the Tone

Faith is not passive. It anticipates. It looks forward with confidence. It says, **"Something good is about to happen."**

That's not hype. That's Kingdom.

Jesus constantly responded to faith. Not need. Not emotions. **Faith.**

- The woman with the issue of blood didn't hope—she believed.
- The centurion told Jesus, "Just say the word."
- Blind Bartimaeus cried out in faith, and Jesus stopped in His tracks.

They received because they expected.

"According to your faith be it unto you."
— Matthew 9:29 (KJV)

You get what you prepare for. You attract what you believe. So ask yourself:

- Am I expecting supernatural provision?
- Am I looking for open doors?
- Am I ready to receive favor, increase, and opportunity?

If not, it's time to raise your expectation.

Declare It—Then Watch for It

As you apply this book's principles, start speaking out what you're believing God for.

Not begging. Declaring.

- "This is a breakthrough year."
- "I am a generous giver, and I live in overflow."

- "My God supplies all my needs and more."
- "I walk in divine provision and supernatural favor."
- "Opportunities are chasing me down."

The power of life and death is in your tongue (Proverbs 18:21). So use it. Don't speak lack and then expect increase. Speak what God says—then watch Him back it up.

Your Testimony Will Set Others Free

This is bigger than you.

As God blesses you, share it. Tell your family. Share it at church. Post it online if the Holy Spirit leads. Your breakthrough isn't just personal—it's prophetic. It tells others, *"If God did it for me, He can do it for you."*

Every testimony becomes a seed of hope for someone else.

That's how the cycle continues:

- You sow in faith.
- God brings breakthrough.
- You testify boldly.
- Others believe and sow in faith.
- God brings more breakthrough.

That's not just momentum—it's revival.

Final Charge: Live Expectant

Close this chapter with conviction: You are not stuck. You are not overlooked. You are not cursed.

You are favored. You are blessed. You are stepping into increase.

Start expecting God to move—not someday, but now. Expect provision. Expect opportunities. Expect miracles. Expect divine connections and open doors.

"Surely goodness and mercy shall follow me all the days of my life..."
— Psalm 23:6

Live like that's true.

Because it is.

CHAPTER 2

How Pastors Can Use This Book to Build Faith in Their People

The Pastor's Role in Teaching Biblical Prosperity

Let's be real—many pastors avoid talking about money. Not because they don't believe in God's provision, but because they've been burned:

- They've been accused of being "money hungry."
- They've had people leave the church over sermons on giving.
- They've seen manipulation disguised as ministry and want no part of it.

So they stay quiet. Play it safe. Mention tithing once in a while, but never go deep.

Here's the problem with that: silence leaves a void, and the world is more than happy to fill it, especially a world filled with social media preachers.

If the Church doesn't teach believers how to think biblically about money, culture will teach them how to fear it, worship it, or mishandle it. And the Church will stay broke—not just financially, but in vision, outreach, and impact.

Why It Matters That You Speak Boldly

Money is spiritual. Jesus talked more about money and possessions than heaven or hell. Not because money is the most important thing—but because how people handle it reveals where their trust really is.

If pastors don't teach this boldly and biblically, people stay bound. Families stay stressed. Generosity stays low. And the Church stays small.

You don't need to manipulate. You don't need to coerce. But you do need to **teach with conviction.** Because this isn't about fundraising. It's about **freedom.**

Freedom from fear.

Freedom from debt.

Freedom to give, build, and bless without limits.

When you teach biblical prosperity, you're not promoting greed—you're unlocking faith.

"So then faith comes by hearing,
and hearing by the word of God."
– Romans 10:17

If people don't hear teaching on provision, how can they believe for it? If they don't believe for it, how can they receive it?

It starts with the pulpit.

Preaching Prosperity vs. Preaching the Kingdom

Some pastors reject anything labeled "prosperity gospel." And rightly so—**if** we're talking about a self-centered, give-to-get, get-rich-off-the-saints distortion.

But let's be clear: **prosperity isn't the gospel—it's a byproduct of the Kingdom.**

When people align their lives with God's ways—faith, obedience, generosity—they will experience increase. That's not hype. That's Bible.

- God blessed Abraham, Isaac, and Jacob with wealth.
- He brought the Israelites out of Egypt with gold and silver.
- He multiplied food and resources for His people time and time again.

Prosperity isn't the goal—it's a tool. The goal is obedience. The goal is impact. Prosperity is simply part of the package when people walk in covenant with God.

So preach the Kingdom—and include provision in it.

Bold Teaching Requires Clean Hands

If you're going to preach boldly, you also need to lead with integrity.

That means:

- Be transparent with church finances.
- Don't teach giving just when the budget's tight.
- Don't use manipulation or guilt.
- Model what you teach—be a giver yourself.

Your boldness will carry more weight when people see your example. And your church will follow the spirit you carry.

Over the many years I've served our church, first as an associate pastor and now for nearly three decades as senior pastor, I've never asked our people to step out in faith in the area of generosity without first leading by example. Whether it was our very first capital campaign, where my wife and I committed to give the equivalent of our tithe on top of our regular giving, or earlier on as an associate pastor when the church faced a financial need, we have always gone first. I still remember a time when, believing God had called us to sow sacrificially, we gave a significant seed from a home equity line of credit (which I wouldn't recommend for everyone). We didn't give recklessly—we gave in faith, convinced that if we led with obedience, God would respond with a harvest. Every seed we've sown has only deepened our conviction: God honors bold, faith-filled generosity.

If you teach with fear, they'll give with fear.

If you teach with faith, they'll give with faith.

You're Not Asking People for Money— You're Leading Them into Breakthrough

When you teach on giving, you're not just trying to meet a budget—you're helping people unlock personal transformation.

Think about it:

- A man burdened by generational poverty gets a vision for financial freedom.
- A single mom learns to trust God with her tithe and watches Him provide week after week.
- A business owner gets clarity on Kingdom wealth and starts funding missions and outreach.

That's breakthrough. And it starts with teaching.

Pastor, you're not just feeding your people spiritually—you're equipping them to win in every area of life. That includes finances. That includes provision.

That includes walking in overflow so they can fulfill their God-given purpose.

Say What Needs to Be Said

Stop letting fear of backlash silence your voice.

- You're not greedy.
- You're not manipulative.
- You're not selling the gospel.

You're teaching God's people how to break free from lack and live under Kingdom supply.

Do it with boldness. Do it with humility. Do it with the Word.

Because when the Church gets this, everything changes.

The Importance of Internal Breakthrough for Pastors

Let's get honest: **A church will never rise higher than the faith of its leader.** If you, as a pastor, are limited in your thinking about finances, your church will live in that same limitation—no matter how much truth you preach from the platform.

You can't lead people into breakthrough you haven't walked in yourself.

And that's not just about income. It's about mindset. Confidence. Boldness. Faith for the impossible. A deep, settled conviction that **God wants to bless His people, and He starts with His leaders.**

Before your church can break through financially, **you must.**

You Can't Afford to Carry a Poverty Mindset

You can preach prosperity all day, but if deep down you believe...

- "I'm not supposed to have too much."
- "People will judge me if I'm blessed."
- "We just need to survive as a church."
- "It's wrong to want financial overflow..."

... then that mindset will leak out in your leadership, your language, and your decisions.

You'll cap the giving culture without even realizing it. You'll unconsciously keep the church in "just enough" mode. You'll fear big vision because deep down, you don't believe provision will follow.

Let's say it clearly: **You can't lead with faith and live with fear.** Something has to shift—and it starts with you.

What Internal Breakthrough Looks Like

Internal breakthrough isn't about driving a luxury car or living in a gated community. It's about freedom.

Boldness. Mental clarity. The ability to say "yes" to what God asks without financial anxiety screaming in the background.

Here's what internal breakthrough produces:

- peace in your finances—even when things are tight,
- faith to believe for supernatural supply—personally and for your church,
- generosity that flows from a place of trust, not obligation,
- vision that isn't limited by the budget,
- confidence to teach prosperity with clean hands and conviction.

It's not about becoming flashy. It's about becoming free.

God Wants to Break You Out—So You Can Lead Others Out

Think about the exodus: God didn't just bring Israel out of Egypt. He brought them out with wealth (Exodus 12:35–36). But first, Moses had to lead the charge—and Moses had to trust God at a deep level before he ever stood before Pharaoh.

Same with you.

You can't preach abundance and live in fear of bills. You can't talk about supernatural provision and shrink back from big asks. You can't encourage people to tithe when you're hesitant in your own giving.

You must lead from experience.

"Follow me, as I follow Christ."
— 1 Corinthians 11:1 (paraphrase)

That applies to finances too.

When your people see you living it—walking in faith, giving boldly, trusting God without apology—it sets a standard they can follow.

Model What You Want to Multiply

You don't reproduce what you teach. You reproduce what you live.

If you want a generous church, model generosity.

If you want a faith-filled culture, show them faith in action.

If you want your church to dream big, cast big vision yourself.

It starts in the pastor's heart. That's where the atmosphere of the church is set.

And don't wait until everything's perfect to step into this. Start now. Even if you're still in process. Even if your church is small or under pressure. Even if you're personally in debt or feel stuck financially.

Internal breakthrough often starts with a decision, not a bank account.

- Decide to believe God's Word about provision.

- Decide to tithe and give sacrificially —consistently.
- Decide to teach your people what you're learning.
- Decide to reject fear and embrace faith.

God honors that kind of leadership.

This Is Bigger Than You

You breaking free financially isn't just for your comfort. It's for your calling.

The vision God has given you requires resources. Staffing. Facilities. Equipment. Outreach. Missions. Training. All of it takes funding. And God isn't just sending people—He's sending partners, provision, and strategy.

But you need to be ready to receive it. That's why internal breakthrough matters.

You're not just stewarding a message. **You're stewarding a movement.** And God needs you free so you can lead with boldness.

Building a Generous Culture in the Church

Your church already has a financial culture. Whether you've been intentional about it or not, there's a shared belief system around giving, provision, and resources that your people operate in.

The question is: **Is that culture Kingdom-aligned? Or is it survival-based?**

Many churches live in a "pay-the-bills" mentality. They budget small, plan safe, and only talk about giving when there's a financial crisis. Generosity becomes a last resort instead of a lifestyle. Vision is limited to what seems affordable. And the members? They follow the same example.

That's not the culture Jesus modeled. And it's not how the Church in Acts operated. They didn't give to keep the lights on—they gave to change the world.

If you want to see supernatural provision, you need to build a supernatural giving culture. As leaders, we are always building culture, whether we realize it or not. The absence of intentionality creates a vacuum, and that vacuum will be filled by someone or something. Over the many years I've led, I've learned this simple truth: If we don't intentionally shape the culture, the most dysfunctional parts of our organization inevitably will. Culture is never neutral; it's always being formed. That's why wise leaders stay vigilant, consistently reinforcing the values, behaviors, and atmosphere they want to see multiplied.

From Obligated Giving to Celebrated Giving

Generosity can't feel like an obligation. It has to become a **joyful act of worship.**

"Each of you should give what you have decided in your heart to give, not reluctantly or under compulsion, for God loves a cheerful giver."
— 2 Corinthians 9:7 (NIV)

If people are giving out of guilt or pressure, the culture is unhealthy. But when giving is celebrated—when it's framed as an opportunity to honor God, change lives, and activate faith—people lean in.

Here's how to shift the tone:

- Celebrate giving moments during service—not as an announcement, but as worship.
- Share stories of what generosity is accomplishing: salvations, missions, families helped, miracles.
- Teach on giving consistently, not reactively.
- Remind people every week: "This isn't about obligation—it's about obedience and opportunity."

The more vision and clarity you give around where offerings go, the more excitement people feel about being part of something bigger than themselves.

Lead With Vision, Not Desperation

Don't lead your church from a deficit mentality. Don't beg people to help "keep the doors open." That kind of messaging reinforces lack and fear. And fear doesn't produce faith—it produces hesitation and control.

Instead, cast vision. Big vision.

- Show what's possible when the church gives generously.
- Paint a picture of what full funding could do in your city.
- Let people see that their giving fuels purpose—not just programs.

Example:

Instead of saying, "We're behind budget this month," say, *"We're believing for full funding so we can launch our outreach center, expand our youth program, and support missionaries. Let's sow into what God wants to do next."*

People don't give to keep the lights on. They give to change lives.

Normalize Generosity

Generosity has to become the norm, not the exception.

Make giving visible in your church culture:

- Share testimonies often. Highlight members who gave and saw God move in powerful ways.
- Celebrate special offerings and giving campaigns.
- Publicly appreciate givers—not by dollar amount, but by heart and faith.

- Teach your leaders, volunteers, and teams that generosity is part of discipleship.

Don't just tell your church to give, show them what a generous life looks like. Start with your leadership team and let it trickle out from there.

Culture doesn't change by announcement. It changes by modeling and repetition.

Generosity Unlocks Breakthrough—Church-Wide

Here's the powerful truth: *A generous church is a blessed church.*

When people give with expectation, faith rises. Needs get met. Projects get funded. Outreach expands. Miracles happen. And the entire church begins to operate with an awareness that *"we're not limited by our budget—we're led by our faith."*

That's when breakthrough begins to multiply. Not just in the church's finances—but in the personal lives of its members.

You're not just trying to get people to be more generous. You're building a culture that expects God to move in response to their obedience.

Practical Ideas to Build a Generous Culture

- Use one of the 52 teachings in this book as a weekly "giving thought" to build faith in your service.

- Share a one-minute testimony during service—someone who saw God move after sowing.
- Take time every few months to teach on generosity as part of your discipleship strategy.
- Include financial faith goals in your annual vision, let people sow into specific Kingdom builders and outreach projects.
- Create ways for people to give beyond tithes (missions, building fund, benevolence, outreach).

The goal is not just more money. The goal is a church full of people who live open-handed—who trust God more than money and are ready to give at any moment.

That kind of church becomes unstoppable.

Breaking Financial Barriers in the Church

Let's talk plainly: *Many churches are stuck financially*—not because God isn't faithful, but because the church is operating with a survival mindset.

Budgets are built on what came in last year, not what the Spirit is calling them to do. Vision is shaped around affordability, not faith. And every dollar spent is treated like a loss, instead of a seed.

That is not how the Kingdom works.

Jesus didn't tell His disciples, "Go into all the world—*as long as the budget allows.*" He sent them with bold instructions and the full backing of heaven. And He's still doing that today.

But to walk in supernatural provision, the church has to *break free from the limitations of a financial stronghold.*

For most of the years I've had the privilege of leading our church, we've experienced consistent financial growth—often in the double digits year after year. Not only were we growing numerically and financially, but also our vision always seemed to outpace both the growth and the needs. As a result, there were many seasons where we paid our bills, but it was tight—sometimes just in time at the end of the month, or even a little into the next.

One day, while meditating on the Scriptures, a very familiar verse came alive in a fresh and powerful way: *"For I am not ashamed of the gospel of Christ, for it is the power of God to salvation for everyone who believes, for the Jew first and also for the Greek."* (Romans 1:16, NKJV). The phrase *"for the Jew first"* leapt off the page.

We had long practiced giving to missions first before paying any of the church's other expenses, but I sensed a prompting from the Holy Spirit: *What if we honored this biblical principle and gave to Jewish evangelism first—before anything else?* I began researching and reaching out to trusted friends to identify ministries that were effectively reaching the descendants of Abraham with the gospel of Jesus Christ.

When we took that step of faith and started giving to Jewish evangelism first, everything changed. Within just a few weeks, we experienced a miraculous shift in the church's finances. Not only were we no longer behind on bills—we began paying them a month in advance! There was no natural explanation for this breakthrough. It was clear that the Lord had revealed a key that unlocked a new level of provision and blessing.

And of course, when the house of God is blessed, it results in more ministry, more evangelism, and more missions going out into the world. It confirmed once again: when we align with God's heart and His Word, supernatural provision follows.

The Survival Mentality: Subtle but Dangerous

Here's what survival mentality sounds like in church leadership:

- "Let's just make sure we don't go into the red this month."
- "We can't afford to do that outreach right now."
- "Let's wait until the giving picks up before we step out."
- "We should lower expectations on this project."
- "We don't want to pressure people by talking about money too much."

None of these seem evil. In fact, they sound responsible. But they're often driven by *fear—not faith.* They put the pressure on what's currently in the account instead of trusting the God of abundance.

A church in survival mode:

- minimizes vision,
- delays obedience,
- avoids bold giving,
- shrinks under pressure.

And worst of all? *It misses out on miracles.*

The Church Must Lead in Faith, Not Mirror the World

If the world is hoarding and playing it safe, the Church should be sowing and stepping out. If the world is full of fear about recessions and inflation, the Church should be a beacon of boldness and provision.

We serve a supernatural God. He's not limited by interest rates, market downturns, or local economic pressure. But if our mindset is limited, we'll never see what He's capable of.

Look at Scripture:

- The Israelites received daily provision in the wilderness.
- Elijah was fed by ravens during a famine.
- The widow's oil didn't run out.

- Jesus paid taxes with a coin from a fish's mouth.
- Thousands were fed with one boy's lunch—and there were leftovers.
- Jesus made more wine than was needed, some would argue even extravagant.

The pattern is clear: *God provides, often in unexpected ways*. But that provision is almost always connected to obedience and faith.

The Enemy Wants the Church to Stay Broke

Let's call it what it is: **Lack is a strategy of the enemy.**

Because a church that's always behind on bills:

- won't send missionaries,
- won't plant churches,
- won't meet needs in their city,
- won't dream big or build,
- won't have influence in the marketplace.

The enemy isn't just after your sermons—he's after your resources. Because if he can keep the Church financially crippled, he can keep it *limited, small, and silent.*

That's why breaking financial barriers is a spiritual battle. It's not just a matter of stewardship—it's about advancing the Kingdom. And it starts with refusing to partner with fear any longer.

Believe Bigger—And Lead Boldly

If your church is going to break out of the cycle of just-enough, it's going to take *faith leadership.*

That doesn't mean being reckless. It means refusing to let lack dictate what your church believes is possible.

Here's what that could look like:

- casting vision beyond your current budget,
- sowing into other ministries even when you're believing for your own breakthrough,
- investing in outreach, missions, and expansion—before the money "makes sense,"
- teaching giving and provision consistently—not just when the church is in a pinch.

God is attracted to faith. And when a church starts operating from bold expectation instead of financial fear, the atmosphere shifts.

People catch the vision. They start giving with faith. Miracles happen. Needs are met. Projects are funded. And a cycle of *Kingdom flow* begins.

Churches That Prioritize Kingdom Giving Will Always Be Provided For

Let's say that again: *Churches that prioritize giving will never lack.*

Why?

Because when you make generosity a priority—not just a principle—you open the flow of heaven.

God trusts givers. He funds vision. He supplies seed to the sower (2 Corinthians 9:10). And when a church is willing to give boldly, even out of its need, God responds with supernatural provision.

There are churches around the world who have lived this:

- giving away massive portions of their income and still ending the year with surplus,
- paying off buildings early,
- supporting full-time missionaries while expanding their own facilities,
- launching major outreaches without taking on debt,
- testifying of checks in the mail, land deals, anonymous donations, and miracle timing.

This isn't fiction—*it's what happens when a church stops living in fear and starts giving like it trusts God.*

And it's possible for your church too.

Strategies for Teaching and Implementing These Principles

Teaching biblical prosperity doesn't require a finance degree—it requires **clarity, consistency, and conviction.** Most pastors believe God wants to bless His people. The problem is they don't always know **how to teach that truth in a way that's bold, biblical, and balanced.**

This section will give you practical strategies to bring these principles into your church culture—not as a one-time message, but as a foundational part of discipleship.

1. Teach Giving Consistently—Not Reactively

One of the biggest mistakes churches make is only teaching about finances when the budget is tight. When giving drops, leaders often scramble to preach on tithing or call for special offerings. But this reactive approach unintentionally trains the church to believe that generosity is only important in times of crisis. The truth is, financial teaching is most effective when it's proactive—when things are going well, not when the pressure is on. If we only speak on giving when we're behind or trying to raise funds, our stress and urgency will inevitably bleed through. And when that happens, we end up doing exactly what Scripture warns against—pressuring people to give. Paul clearly tells us not to give "under compulsion or necessity," because God loves a cheerful giver. Teaching under pressure might produce a short-term bump, but it undermines trust and sabotages long-term generosity. Instead, cultivate a culture of cheerful, faith-filled giving by teaching biblical financial principles consistently and confidently, regardless of the current financial season.

Teach about generosity, stewardship, provision, and financial faith as part of your regular rhythm—just like you teach about prayer, salvation, and forgiveness.

Consistency builds culture. When giving is normalized and celebrated year-round, it becomes a part of how your church thinks, not just how it responds.

2. Use This Book as a Teaching Foundation

Don't reinvent the wheel—use this book as a guide. Here are a few ideas:

- **Sunday Series:** Preach a message series based on the teachings in this book. Each week, unpack a principle—faith, obedience, sowing, breaking poverty mindsets—and give your congregation space to apply it.
- **Small Group Curriculum:** Break the book into weekly discussions with study guides and prayer prompts.
- **Leadership Development:** Walk your leadership team through the book section by section. Let

them get it in their spirit first, so they can help model it to the rest of the church.

- **Church-Wide Campaign:** Take your whole church through a 21-day or 40-day "Faith and Finances" journey using the book, daily devotionals, and testimonies.

The goal isn't to just give information—it's to **build momentum.** When everyone is focused on faith and provision together, unity and expectation rise.

3. Shift from Guilt-Based Giving to Faith-Filled Giving

If people give because they feel bad, they're giving from the wrong place. That kind of giving is short-term and unfruitful. It may solve a temporary budget need, but it won't change hearts.

The Bible says:

"Each one must give as he has decided in his heart, not reluctantly or under compulsion."
— 2 Corinthians 9:7 (ESV)

Guilt is manipulation. *Faith is motivation.*

So instead of saying, "We really need everyone to give today," say, "We have an opportunity to activate our faith through generosity—and we're believing God for big things."

Faith-filled giving is expectant. It's joyful. It's rooted in trust, not pressure.

Train your team to talk about giving this way. Model it in how you frame the offering. And always connect generosity to vision, not obligation.

4. Create Opportunities to Give Beyond the Tithe

Most people in your church will tithe (or want to), but they don't always have clear places to sow above and beyond. If you want to grow a generous culture, create space for radical giving.

Here are a few ideas:

- **Missions Giving:** Set up recurring support for missionaries or organizations—and let people give toward that monthly.
- **Outreach Projects:** Build momentum around local outreach, food drives, school support, or community events.
- **Church Building Fund:** Whether you're renovating, buying land, or just preparing for the future, let people sow into the expansion of God's house.
- **Benevolence Fund:** Give your church the opportunity to help families in crisis directly.

Let people give toward **vision, not just bills.** When the giving becomes about Kingdom advancement, hearts open and hands follow.

5. Use Testimonies to Reinforce Teaching

One of your greatest teaching tools is the **testimony of your people.** When someone steps out in faith and sees God provide, share it. When someone pays off debt, gets a raise after giving, or receives supernatural provision—tell the story.

Don't keep financial miracles private. Celebrate them publicly (with permission).

It does a few things:

- It makes the message real.
- It builds collective faith.
- It shows your church that these principles work in real life.

You can do this through:

- a short video testimony during the service,
- a written story in your weekly email or bulletin,
- a quick live interview before or after the offering.

Make it normal to talk about money miracles in your church—not in a flashy way, but in a **faith-building way.**

Final Thought: Simplicity Over Complexity

You don't need to preach like a financial expert. You don't need to teach like a stockbroker. You just need to clearly communicate what God's Word says and show your church how to live it.

People don't need complicated systems. They need:

- faith that God is their Provider,
- obedience in tithing and giving,
- confidence that generosity brings breakthrough,
- real examples of how it's working in their church.

Teach it simply. Teach it often. Teach it like you believe it. And watch what happens in your congregation.

6. Leading the Church into a New Level of Faith

Faith is not just something your church talks about — it's something your church is called to **live in**. And if you want to see lasting financial breakthrough in your people, it won't happen through information alone. It takes **leadership** that's willing to call them higher.

This isn't about hype. It's about building a church that moves by faith, gives with boldness, and expects God to do the impossible.

If you want to shift your church from maintenance mode to Kingdom momentum, you've got to lead the way.

Challenge the Congregation to Stretch Their Faith

Most people don't need another reminder to tithe. They need a reason to believe bigger.

They need to be invited to:

- give when it doesn't make sense,
- believe for supernatural supply in hard seasons,
- expect financial miracles,
- see money as a tool for impact, not just survival.

If all your teaching stays safe and manageable, people will stay in their comfort zones. But when you preach faith, model faith, and challenge your church to **stretch their obedience**, they start to grow.

Don't be afraid to challenge them.

- Preach bold messages that stir expectation.
- Ask them to pray about sacrificial giving.
- Invite them to trust God on a new level — even if it's uncomfortable.

God meets people at their faith, not at their convenience.

"According to your faith be it unto you."
— Matthew 9:29 (KJV)

So give them a reason to believe big.

Hold Special Prayer Services for Financial Breakthrough

One of the most powerful things you can do is gather your church to pray — *specifically for financial breakthrough.*

You pray for healing. You pray for revival. Why not provision?

Set aside time for focused prayer on:

- debt cancellation
- job provision and promotions
- business success and open doors
- supernatural strategy and increase
- freedom from financial fear and stress
- wisdom in stewardship

Lay hands on people. Anoint business owners. Pray over offering envelopes. Create moments of encounter around this area — because for many, money is the greatest source of anxiety in their lives.

When they see that God cares about this part of their life, it opens the door for greater trust and obedience.

Breakthrough often starts in prayer.

Cast a Clear Vision for the Church's Financial Future

People don't just give to problems — they give to vision.

If you want your church to rise to a new level of giving, you need to give them a picture of **where you're going**. Be specific. Be clear. And be bold.

Cast vision for:

- a debt-free church
- a fully staffed, fully resourced ministry team
- building ownership and expansion
- a church that tithes on its income and sows into other churches
- outreaches that bless your city at scale
- generosity that flows globally through missions and church plants

Then connect giving to the vision. Make it tangible: *"Every time you give, you're helping build this future."*

People want to know their giving matters. Show them that it does.

"Write the vision and make it plain."
— Habakkuk 2:2

Clarity produces movement. When people can see what their generosity unlocks, they'll rise to the challenge.

Operate in Faith, Not Fear — Even Before You See the Results

This is where leadership gets real.

You may not see all the provision yet. You may still be behind on the budget. You may feel the pressure to play it safe. But the call of God is still this:

Lead by faith.

Speak faith.

Plan by faith.

Give by faith.

Call your people to faith.

Don't wait until the books look good to start believing. Breakthrough often comes **after** obedience — not before. And if you lead with fear, your church will follow with hesitation.

So even if your situation hasn't shifted yet:

- Preach like breakthrough is happening.
- Cast vision like the budget is already met.
- Thank God in advance for the harvest.

Faith isn't about denial — it's about *declaring what God says is possible.*

And when your people see you lead this way, they'll follow.

Final Charge: Build a Church That Expects Supernatural Provision

You're not just running a church. You're stewarding a movement. And movements require resources.

So stop apologizing for believing God can provide more.

Stop pulling back on vision because of finances.

Stop underestimating the generosity of your people.

Start leading with supernatural expectation.

- Expect surplus.
- Expect growth.
- Expect breakthrough in the lives of your people.
- Expect to give more than you've ever given.
- Expect to be a testimony that builds faith across your city.

Because when you raise the level of faith in your church, God responds. And what you'll see won't just be a financial turnaround — it'll be a spiritual shift.

1.

Giving Begins with the Heart

Scripture: 2 Corinthians 9:7

"So let each one give as he purposes in his heart,
not grudgingly or of necessity;
for God loves a cheerful giver."

Giving isn't about pressure—it's about passion! The Apostle Paul makes it clear that giving should never be done out of reluctance or obligation. Instead, it's an expression of our heart, our love for God, and our trust in His provision. When we give, we're not losing something; we're stepping into a powerful Kingdom principle—**sowing and reaping.**

Too often, people give hesitantly, as if they're parting with something they can't afford to lose. But that's a scarcity mindset! We don't give to get rid of money; we give because we love God, love His house, and love seeing lives transformed through the power of the gospel. A heart that's surrendered to God is a heart that gives freely. When we give with joy, heaven takes notice.

Tithing Is the Start—Generosity Is the Lifestyle

The tithe is already God's—it's the baseline of biblical obedience. But **true generosity begins where the**

tithe ends. That's when the fun starts! When we give above and beyond, we're showing God that He has our heart, not just our leftovers. And here's the thing—God **never** takes from us; He sets us up for supernatural increase!

We don't give out of fear or obligation; we give because **we love to give, and we live to give.** Giving is a privilege. It's a way we partner with God to see His Kingdom expand, souls saved, churches built, and communities transformed.

When you live with an open hand, you position yourself for an overflow. You can't outgive God! When you sow generously, you reap abundantly—because **God loves a cheerful giver!**

PowerPoint:

We LOVE TO GIVE — We LIVE TO GIVE!

2.

Refreshing and Generosity

Scripture: Proverbs 11:25 (NLT)

"The generous will prosper; those who refresh others will themselves be refreshed."

Generosity is a game-changer! When we step into a life of open-handed giving, we align ourselves with a divine principle—**blessing flows through those who give.** The Bible is clear: generosity isn't just about meeting needs; it's about stepping into **God's economy.** Those who pour out, **God pours back into.** Those who refresh others, **God refreshes.**

Some people hesitate when it comes to generosity because they think it will leave them with less. But God's Kingdom doesn't work like that! The world says, "Hold on tight," but **God says, "Give, and it will come back to you!"** The generous will prosper—not maybe, not sometimes—WILL.

Prosperity and Refreshing Go Hand in Hand

Two key principles emerge from this passage:

1. **Generosity brings increase** – When we live with an open hand, God blesses what we release. You can't be a generous person and stay in lack. God

sees to it that **those who give will always have more to give!**

2. **Refreshing comes to the generous** – It's impossible to give and not receive in return. There's something supernatural that happens when we invest in others. We don't just bless others—we get **filled, revived, and strengthened** ourselves.

Sowing into nations:

In 1998 as a brand-new senior pastor, the Lord clearly spoke to me: "If you sow into the nations, I will give you a city."

As a church, we don't just give—we sow. Every time we bring the tithe, every time we give to missions, every time we bless ministries around the world, we are making an **eternal impact.** And God's promise is clear: When we give beyond ourselves, He moves **in our midst.**

This isn't just about financial blessing—this is about **revival. When we sow into nations, we reap cities for Jesus.** We believe that as we live generously, we will see not just financial breakthrough but a powerful **outpouring of the Holy Spirit.**

PowerPoint:

Each week as we bring the tithe and give, we are sowing into nations, and we believe we will not only see our cities won for Jesus but also experience an outpouring of His refreshing!

3.

Practicing Consistent and Systematic Giving

Scripture: 1 Corinthians 16:1–2 (The Message)

"Regarding the relief offering for poor Christians that is being collected, you get the same instructions I gave the churches in Galatia. Every Sunday each of you make an offering and put it in safekeeping. Be as generous as you can. When I get there, you'll have it ready, and I won't have to make a special appeal."

One of the marks of a **strong and mature church** is its commitment to **consistent and systematic giving.** Paul was instructing the Corinthian believers not to wait for a last-minute appeal but to prepare their giving in advance. This principle is just as relevant today as it was then. **A church that gives intentionally and generously never lacks!**

Too often, people wait to give until they feel emotionally moved by a special need. But Paul is saying, **don't wait—plan to give!** The strength of a church isn't measured just by its worship or preaching but by its generosity. **A giving church is a thriving church.**

Key Principles from Paul's Instruction:

1. **Giving is above the tithe** – Paul was talking about a relief offering on top of regular tithes. The tithe belongs to the Lord, but generosity starts beyond the tithe.
2. **Generosity is the standard** – Paul didn't set a minimum amount—he encouraged each person to give as much as they could. The focus wasn't on equal giving but on equal sacrifice.
3. **Giving should be consistent and systematic** – Paul instructed them to set aside their giving every Sunday, ensuring that there would be no need for a last-minute appeal. When giving becomes a lifestyle, God's house never lacks, and the work of ministry flourishes.

A Healthy Church Is a Giving Church

A **healthy and spiritual church** doesn't rely on crisis appeals or emotional giving—it operates on **faithful, consistent, and systematic generosity.** When people plan their giving, the church can expand its reach, support missions, and provide for those in need without financial strain.

The key to a **blessed life** and a **strong church** is to give regularly, generously, and intentionally. We don't give when it's convenient—we give **because it's who we are!**

PowerPoint:

The healthy and spiritual church is: generous, consistent, and systematic in giving to God's work.

4.

The Lord Is Magnified When You Are Blessed

Scripture: Psalm 35:27

"Let them shout for joy and be glad, who favor my righteous cause; and let them say continually, 'Let the Lord be magnified, Who has pleasure in the prosperity of His servant.'"

God is not against blessing—**He is for it!** The Bible is clear: God **takes pleasure** in the prosperity of His people. Religion has often painted prosperity as something negative, but the Word of God tells a different story. **God delights in blessing His children!** When we prosper, it's not just for our own comfort or gain—it's so that His name is magnified, and His Kingdom advances.

Prosperity with a Purpose

The world teaches that prosperity is about **self-gain**, but in the Kingdom of God, prosperity is about purpose. God blesses us so that we can be a blessing. If our heart is aligned with His, we will see prosperity as a tool, not a trophy. **It's a means to an end—and that end is world evangelism.**

Key Truths About Prosperity in the Kingdom:

1. **God has no problem blessing you.** He actually enjoys it! He is a good Father who desires to see His children thrive.

2. **Prosperity is for a greater purpose.** It's not just about personal success—it's about making a global impact. When God increases us, it's so we can fund the gospel, build churches, and reach the lost.

3. **Your prosperity magnifies God.** When believers walk in blessing and use their resources for the Kingdom, it testifies to the world that God is a good provider. It shows that we serve a God of abundance, not lack.

We Prosper to Preach the Gospel

We must always remember: Prosperity is not the goal—souls are the goal. Every financial breakthrough, every business success, and every increase is an opportunity to push the gospel further. The more we have, the more we can give.

As we **bring our tithes, sow our offerings, and walk in financial blessing**, we are fueling the greatest mission on earth—seeing people come to Jesus!

PowerPoint:

God is magnified when we prosper BECAUSE we use it to preach the gospel all around the world!

5.

The Many Blessings of the Lord

Scripture: Deuteronomy 28:1–2 (ESV)

"And if you faithfully obey the voice of the Lord your God, being careful to do all his commandments that I command you today, the Lord your God will set you high above all the nations of the earth. And all these blessings shall come upon you and overtake you, if you obey the voice of the Lord your God."

God is a **God of blessing**, and He has laid out a clear principle in His Word: **Obedience leads to blessing.** The passage in Deuteronomy tells us that when we listen to His voice and obey His Word, blessings don't just come to us—they overtake us! That means we don't have to chase after blessing; blessing chases after us when we walk in obedience.

Obedience Unlocks Blessing

Many people wonder why they aren't seeing God's provision and favor in their lives, yet they hesitate when it comes to obeying Him—especially in the area of giving. The Bible is clear: When we honor God's principles, we position ourselves to **walk in His promises.**

Two Ways We Obey the Voice of God:

1. **Through His Written Word** – The Bible already gives us clear instructions on how to live, including the principle of tithing. Malachi 3:10 tells us to bring the whole tithe into the storehouse—this is non-negotiable for a believer who wants to walk in blessing.
2. **Through His Spoken Word** – The Holy Spirit still speaks today, leading us to sow offerings in specific places. There are moments when God asks us to step out in faith and give beyond the tithe, and when we obey, He responds with supernatural provision.

Living in the Overflow of Blessing

God's blessings are **not just financial**; they touch every area of our lives—our health, our families, our businesses, and our influence. When we follow His commands, He positions us **for increase, promotion, and abundance.**

When we bring the tithe, we are simply returning to God what already belongs to Him. But true generosity begins where the tithe ends. That's when we step into a new level of faith, allowing God to bless us **beyond what we could ask or imagine.**

PowerPoint:

When you obey His voice, you will walk in the promise of blessings!

6.

Give Thanks to the Lord

Scripture: Psalm 136:1–3

"Oh, give thanks to the Lord, for He is good!
For His mercy endures forever.

Oh, give thanks to the God of gods!
For His mercy endures forever.

Oh, give thanks to the Lord of lords!
For His mercy endures forever."

Gratitude is one of the most powerful attitudes a believer can carry. The Bible repeatedly tells us to **give thanks to the Lord**—not just with our words but through our actions. True thanksgiving isn't just what we say, it's what we do.

Giving Is an Act of Thanksgiving

When we bring our tithe and offerings, we are demonstrating our gratitude to God. We are saying, *"Lord, I recognize that everything I have comes from You. My ability to work, my finances, my health, and my success—it's all because of Your grace and mercy."*

A **thankful person is a giving person.** Someone who truly understands the goodness of God will naturally live generously. Why? Because they recognize that they are already blessed, and they want to honor God with what they have.

Three Ways Giving Expresses Our Thankfulness:

1. **We acknowledge God's provision** – By tithing and giving, we declare that God is our source, not our job, not the economy, not our efforts.
2. **We honor His mercy and grace** – Every blessing we have is because of His mercy. Giving is our way of saying *"Thank You, Lord, for Your faithfulness in my life!"*
3. **We show obedience through an open hand** – A closed hand reveals a heart that doesn't trust God. But an open hand says, *"Lord, I trust You, and I give freely because I know You will always take care of me."*

Thankfulness Separates the Giver from the Non-Giver

Some people live life **always wanting more** but never releasing what they have. That's not thankfulness—that's selfishness! A truly grateful person gives because they recognize they are already **blessed beyond measure.**

When we give, we are positioning ourselves for **even greater blessing.** The more we express gratitude through generosity, the more God entrusts us with His abundance.

PowerPoint:

A giving person is a thankful person—a non-giving person is an unthankful person to the Lord.

7.

Honoring God with the First

Scripture: Proverbs 3:9–10

"Honor the Lord with your possessions, and with the firstfruits of all your increase; so your barns will be filled with plenty, and your vats will overflow with new wine."

Honoring God is about priorities. It's about putting Him first in every area of our lives—including our finances. The principle of first fruits is more than just a financial act; it's a spiritual declaration that God is our source and our trust is in Him, not in our money or resources.

Why First Matters to God

God doesn't want to be second. Throughout Scripture, He commands us to bring the first—the firstborn, the first fruits, the first portion—because **what we do first reveals what we truly trust in.**

Tithing isn't just about giving; it's about honoring. When we bring the first tenth of our income to God, we are saying, "Lord, You come first in my life. I trust You before I trust anything else."

The Blessing of Putting God First

God attaches a promise to putting Him first:

1. **Provision and Abundance** – "Your barns will be filled with plenty." When we put God first in our finances, He makes sure that we never lack. Tithing isn't about subtraction—it's about multiplication!
2. **Fresh Anointing and Overflow** – "Your vats will overflow with new wine." Wine represents the anointing and favor of God. When we honor Him first, He releases fresh wisdom, opportunity, and supernatural blessing into our lives.

Honoring God Through Tithing

Some people give after they've paid their bills, bought their groceries, and handled all their expenses. But that's not honoring God with the first. **Giving first is an act of faith.** It says, "Lord, I trust You to bless the rest because *I'm putting You first.*"

When we **prioritize the Kingdom,** we position ourselves for blessing. The tithe is not about what we give; it's about **who we put first.**

PowerPoint:

Bringing to God the tithe first is how we honor Him.

8.

Gratefulness

Scripture: Luke 17:11–18 (ESV)

"On the way to Jerusalem he was passing along between Samaria and Galilee. And as he entered a village, he was met by ten lepers, who stood at a distance and lifted up their voices, saying, 'Jesus, Master, have mercy on us.' When he saw them he said to them, 'Go and show yourselves to the priests.' And as they went they were cleansed. Then one of them, when he saw that he was healed, turned back, praising God with a loud voice; and he fell on his face at Jesus' feet, giving him thanks. Now he was a Samaritan. Then Jesus answered, 'Were not ten cleansed? Where are the nine? Was no one found to return and give praise to God except this foreigner?'"

Gratefulness is a key principle in the Kingdom of God. In this story, ten men received physical healing, but only one took the time to come back to Jesus and express his thankfulness. The tragedy? Nine walked away with healed bodies but ungrateful hearts. They received their miracle, but they **missed the deeper blessing of connection with Jesus.**

Gratitude Unlocks More

Gratitude is more than good manners—it's **a posture of the heart** that attracts **greater blessing.** When we take time to thank God for what He has done, we position ourselves for even more of His goodness.

- **Grateful people are entrusted with more** – When we acknowledge what God has done, He knows He can trust us with greater things.
- **A lack of gratitude leads to spiritual deformity** – The nine lepers were physically healed but spiritually lacking. Gratitude isn't just about saying "thank you"—it's about recognizing that every good thing comes from God.
- **Giving thanks is an act of worship** – The one leper who returned didn't just say thank you—he fell at Jesus's feet in worship. True gratitude leads us into a deeper relationship with God.

Thankfulness and Generosity Go Hand in Hand

When we are grateful, we naturally live generously. Ungrateful people are often the most reluctant to give because they fail to recognize how much they've already received. But when we acknowledge that **everything we have is from God,** we can't help but give back to Him **with joy.**

Every time we **tithe, sow, or serve,** we are expressing our gratitude. We are saying, "Lord, I recognize

Your hand in my life, and I honor You with what I have."

PowerPoint:

Gratefulness brings us into greater blessing.

9.

Preparing Yourself to Receive

Scripture: 2 Corinthians 9:6

"But this I say: He who sows sparingly will also reap sparingly, and he who sows bountifully will also reap bountifully."

Giving and receiving are spiritual laws that work just like the laws of **sowing and reaping in agriculture.** The Apostle Paul used this analogy because farming is something people understood—you can't expect a harvest if you haven't planted any seed!

Many believers struggle with receiving because they haven't truly embraced this principle. God's Word doesn't just teach us to **give**—it also teaches us to **expect a return.** Some hesitate to believe for a harvest because they don't want to seem selfish. But Scripture is clear: **God set this law in motion!** A farmer doesn't plant seeds without expecting a harvest, and we shouldn't give without faith that God will bring increase.

The Biblical Principle of Sowing and Reaping

1. **You must sow to reap**—If nothing is planted, nothing will grow. Some people want bless-

ing without generosity, but that's not how the Kingdom works!

2. **Sowing determines the size of the harvest**—Paul said those who sow sparingly will reap sparingly, but those who sow bountifully will reap bountifully. The measure we use determines the measure we receive.

3. **Receiving isn't our motivation**—it's God's principle. We don't give just to get, but we recognize that God honors giving with increase. Putting Him first in our finances aligns us with His system of supernatural provision.

Positioning Yourself for God's Best

God is looking for people He can trust with more. If He knows we will be faithful with what He puts in our hands, He will continue to pour out provision. The issue is **not whether God can bless us—but whether we are ready to receive it.**

- Are we **faithful sowers?**
- Do we **expect God's promises** to manifest?
- Are we **positioning ourselves in faith** for the harvest?

The Key to Kingdom Increase

We will only ever get out of the field what we put into it. A farmer doesn't wait for crops to appear before planting—he sows in faith, knowing the harvest will come. In the same way, we must give in faith, trusting that God's principles are true.

PowerPoint:

The only way we get something out of the field is to put something into it.

10.

The Lord Owns It All

Scripture: Psalm 24:1

"The earth is the Lord's, and all its fullness,
The world and those who dwell therein."

One of the greatest revelations we can have as believers is that **we own nothing—God owns it all!** Everything in this world belongs to Him: our resources, our finances, our talents, and even our very breath. We are not owners; we are stewards.

Stewardship vs. Ownership

Many people struggle with letting go of their resources because they view what they have as theirs. But the moment we realize that **God owns everything**, we step into a **different mindset—a stewardship mindset.**

A steward manages what belongs to someone else. Our job is to manage well what God has put into our hands, whether that's our finances, businesses, or opportunities. **When we take care of what belongs to God, He can entrust us with more!**

Because He Owns It All, We Do Not Have to Lack

If God owns everything, then we lack nothing! He is not just the owner of the earth—**He is the God of abundance!**

- **God is our Source** – We don't have to strive or worry about provision because our Father owns it all.
- **God is the God of more than enough** – He never just provides the bare minimum. He is the God of overflow.
- **When we trust His ownership, we step into blessing** – Instead of living with a scarcity mindset, we live with an expectation of increase.

Expressing Our Trust Through Tithing and Giving

When we bring the Lord's tithe and give our offerings, we are not just fulfilling a duty—we are making a declaration of faith. We are saying:

- *"Lord, I recognize that everything I have belongs to You."*
- *"I trust You as my provider, not my job or my bank account."*
- *"I choose to manage Your resources well, and I know You will bless and multiply them."*

Positioning for Supernatural Increase

When we steward well what belongs to God, we make room for Him to do the impossible. We open the door for supernatural favor, abundance, and divine provision. **The more we surrender to God's ownership, the more we see His hand move in our lives.**

PowerPoint:

As we are good stewards of what is God's, we make room for Him to do exceedingly abundantly beyond all that we could ask or think—because it all belongs to Him!

11.

God Multiplies What Is Given to Him in Faith

Scripture: John 6:5–9 (ESV)

"Lifting up his eyes, then, and seeing that a large crowd was coming toward him, Jesus said to Philip, 'Where are we to buy bread, so that these people may eat?' He said this to test him, for he himself knew what he would do. Philip answered him, 'Two hundred denarii worth of bread would not be enough for each of them to get a little.' One of his disciples, Andrew, Simon Peter's brother, said to him, 'There is a boy here who has five barley loaves and two fish, but what are they for so many?'"

One of the most powerful principles of the Kingdom is that God multiplies what we give to Him in faith. This story of Jesus feeding the multitude is a clear demonstration of how faith-filled giving produces supernatural increase.

Faith Sees Opportunity, Not Lack

When the disciples saw the size of the crowd, they saw lack. Philip immediately calculated the cost and determined that there was no way they could feed everyone. But Jesus already knew what He would do—

He was simply waiting for someone to **place something in His hands.**

Often, when it comes to giving, we fall into the same mindset as Philip:

- *"I don't have enough to make a difference."*
- *"What I have isn't significant."*
- *"I need to hold on to what I have."*

But Kingdom **multiplication doesn't start with what we don't have—it starts with what we are willing to give in faith!**

The Power of a Small Seed in God's Hands

It wasn't a wealthy person who stepped up that day—it was a boy with five loaves and two fish. In the natural, it looked insignificant, but in the hands of Jesus, it became more than enough.

- **The small offering fed 20,000-25,000 people** (including women and children).
- **There were twelve baskets of leftovers**—one for each disciple!

What does this teach us?

1. God doesn't need a large amount—He needs our obedience and faith.
2. When we give, we activate the principle of supernatural multiplication.

3. There is always overflow when we trust God with what we have.

Giving in Faith Activates the Miraculous

The miracle didn't happen while the boy was holding his lunch—it happened when he **placed it in Jesus's hands.** The same is true with our giving. We can either hold on to what we have, or we can release it in faith and watch God multiply it.

Every time we **tithe, sow, or give**, we are taking our natural resource and placing it into the hands of a supernatural God. What seems small in our hands becomes **more than enough** in His.

PowerPoint:

What we give may not seem like a lot in the big scope of things, but when we give it in faith, God multiplies it!

12.

More than Enough

Scripture: 2 Corinthians 9:8 (RSV)

"And God is able to provide you with every blessing in abundance, so that you may always have enough of everything and may provide in abundance for every good work."

God is not a God of just barely enough—He is the God of more than enough! The Apostle Paul reminds us in this passage that God's provision isn't just about meeting our needs, but about positioning us to be a blessing to others.

Abundance with a Purpose

Many people misunderstand the idea of prosperity in the Kingdom. Biblical prosperity isn't about selfish gain—it's about Kingdom impact. God doesn't bless us just so we can be comfortable—He blesses us so we can bless others.

- **God provides in abundance** – His plan has always been overflow, not lack. When we walk in His provision, we are positioned to be generous in every season.
- **If God can get it THROUGH me, He will get it TO me** – God is looking for people who will

be channels of blessing, not just containers. The more we are willing to release, the more God will pour into our lives.

- **We are blessed to be a blessing** – This principle started with Abraham in Genesis 12 and still applies today. God told Abraham: *"I will bless you... and you shall be a blessing."* That same promise is for us—we are blessed so we can advance the Kingdom, support the church, and impact lives.

Stepping into a Life of Abundance

Abundance isn't just about money—it's about **having enough of everything:**

Enough peace to encourage others.

Enough wisdom to guide others.

Enough provision to be generous in every good work.

When we understand that God's blessing has a purpose, we stop holding back. We tithe in faith, give generously, and sow expectantly, knowing that God will always provide more than enough for every assignment He calls us to.

PowerPoint:

If God can get it THROUGH me, He will get it TO me!

13.

Our Giving Goes Around the World

Scripture: Romans 10:15

"And how shall they preach unless they are sent? As it is written: 'How beautiful are the feet of those who preach the gospel of peace, who bring glad tidings of good things!'"

When we give, we are **sending the gospel** to places we may never physically go. Our giving is not just about keeping the church running—it is about fueling the mission of Jesus Christ. The church is the **God-ordained channel** through which the gospel reaches the nations.

Giving Is Sending

- Every time we bring our **tithe and offerings**, we are directly **supporting the work of evangelism.**
- Our giving allows pastors, **missionaries, and ministries** to go and preach the gospel.
- We are part of something bigger than ourselves—**we are co-laborers in the harvest of souls!**

Some may never stand behind a pulpit, travel to a mission field, or plant a church—but when we give, we are part of every soul that is saved, every church that is built, and every life that is transformed.

The Multiplication Effect of Giving

1. **We give to the local church** – The local church is God's design for equipping believers and spreading the gospel.
2. **Our giving sends the gospel globally** – Churches partner with missions, ministries, and outreaches to bring the message of Jesus to unreached places.
3. **God brings the increase** – As we faithfully give, God multiplies the impact, opening more doors and reaching more people.
4. **We do it again** – The cycle continues: as the church reaches more people, more souls are saved, and more resources are needed to continue the mission.

The Eternal Impact of Our Giving

Giving isn't just financial—it's eternal. When we invest in God's Kingdom, we are investing in people's salvation, in changed lives, in families restored, and in nations transformed. The gospel is going forth because of our obedience in giving.

PowerPoint:

We can give to God through the local church—it goes around the world—God brings the increase—and we do it over again!

14.

Food in the House

Scripture: Malachi 3:10

"Bring all the tithes into the storehouse, that there may be food in My house, and try Me now in this," says the Lord of hosts, "If I will not open for you the windows of heaven and pour out for you such blessing that there will not be room enough to receive it."

The Tithe Belongs to the Lord

Tithing is not about **giving God a portion of what is ours**—it's about **returning to God what is already His.** The Bible makes it clear:

- The tithe does not belong to us; it belongs to the Lord.
- Because it belongs to Him, He has the authority to tell us where to bring it—to the storehouse, which is the local church.

Why the Storehouse?

1. **The Storehouse is the Local Church** – In biblical times, the storehouse was where the resources for God's people were kept. Today, the church is the place where believers are spiritually fed,

equipped, and empowered to carry out the work of the Kingdom.

2. **Tithing Provides Spiritual Food** – The primary purpose of bringing the tithe is that there would be food in God's house. This means:
   - **The needs of the church are met**—the mission moves forward, lives are changed, and the gospel is preached.
   - **Spiritual nourishment flows**—people receive the Word, revelation, and the power of God's presence.

Tithing Opens the Windows of Heaven

This is the only place in Scripture where God says, *"Try Me now in this."* He is inviting us to put His Word to the test.

- When we obey in tithing, He promises to open the windows of heaven over our lives.
- He doesn't just provide—He pours out more than enough!

We Are Blessed to Be a Blessing

Tithing ensures that we are fed spiritually, but it also empowers the church to **feed others**—physically and spiritually. The cycle of blessing continues:

- As we bring the tithe, **we are nourished.**
- As the church is nourished, **we are able to reach more people.**

- The more people are reached, **the more the Kingdom grows!**

PowerPoint:

We BRING the Tithe that BELONGS to Him to HIS HOUSE... and God's promise is that we will continually be fed and be able to feed... and reach the world!

15.

God's Way

Scripture: Isaiah 55:8 (ESV)

"For my thoughts are not your thoughts, neither are your ways my ways," declares the Lord.

One of the greatest revelations we can have as believers is that **God's ways are higher than our ways.** The way the **world thinks about money, resources, and success is vastly different from how God's Kingdom operates.**

God's Principles of Giving and Receiving

1. **Tithing and giving were instituted by God—not for His sake, but for ours.**
    - God doesn't need our money—He is the Creator of everything!
    - He set up the principle of giving to position us for provision and blessing.
2. **Giving is not about losing—it's about gaining.**
    - Many people resist giving because they believe it takes away from them.
    - But God never takes from us—He sets us up for increase!
3. **Our giving is a seed that produces harvest.**

- When we release what's in our hand, God releases what's in His.
- Giving doesn't just bring provision into our own lives—it also fuels Kingdom work around the world.

Kingdom Economics vs. World Economics

The world says: "Hold on to what you have, because you might lose it."
God says: "Give, and watch Me multiply it!"
Luke 6:38 (ESV)

"Give, and it will be given to you. Good measure, pressed down, shaken together, running over, will be put into your lap. For with the measure you use it will be measured back to you."

This verse reveals that giving is a cycle:

- What we give, God multiplies back.
- The measure we use determines the measure we receive.
- Giving is the key to supernatural overflow.

Breaking Free from a Scarcity Mindset

God's way of provision is **faith-driven, not fear-driven.** When we try to hold onto everything, we are operating from a **spirit of fear and lack.** But when we trust God and release what we have, we step into abundance and supernatural supply.

Tithing, giving, and sowing into God's Kingdom are **not about loss but about positioning.** It's about stepping into God's way of financial breakthrough.

PowerPoint:

God's ways are to bless us and use us to reach the world. Man's way says, "Hold on to everything you have"—God says, "Release what's in your hand, and I'll release what's in My hand."

16.

The Principle of Eternal Investments

Scripture: Matthew 6:19–21

"Do not lay up for yourselves treasures on earth, where moth and rust destroy and where thieves break in and steal; but lay up for yourselves treasures in heaven, where neither moth nor rust destroys and where thieves do not break in and steal. For where your treasure is, there your heart will be also."

Investing in What Truly Matters

Jesus isn't saying that wealth is wrong or that we shouldn't be wise with our finances. Instead, He's teaching us about priorities. It's not a matter of **having wealth**, but rather **where we invest it.**

The world tells us to **accumulate, save, and protect our assets**—but Jesus calls us to invest in eternity. He contrasts two kinds of investments:

1. **Earthly Investments** – These are temporary, subject to loss, decay, and theft. No matter how much we store up, it remains fragile and uncertain.
2. **Heavenly Investments** – These are eternal and can never be lost, stolen, or destroyed. When

we invest in the Kingdom, we are storing up treasures that will last forever.

Where Your Treasure Is, Your Heart Will Follow

Jesus makes a profound statement: Our heart follows our treasure, not the other way around.

- If we want a greater passion for the Kingdom, we need to invest in the Kingdom.
- If we invest more in temporary things, our heart will be attached to things that won't last.
- If we sow into God's work, our heart will be aligned with His eternal purposes.

Kingdom Investments Yield Eternal Dividends

The things we give to God—our tithes, offerings, generosity toward missions and the poor—are not just financial transactions. They are eternal investments that bring Kingdom impact.

- Earthly investments fade, but Kingdom investments last forever.
- A heart set on eternity is a heart positioned for supernatural provision.
- What we give today will be producing fruit long after we're gone.

Sowing into the Kingdom

Every act of giving is a seed sown into eternity. When we give to support the local church, missions, outreach, and ministry work, we are storing up treasures in heaven.

PowerPoint:

What I invest in the Kingdom has eternal dividends.

17.

Cheerful Givers

Scripture: 2 Corinthians 9:7

"So let each one give as he purposes in his heart, not grudgingly or of necessity; for God loves a cheerful giver."

Giving with the Right Heart

God isn't just concerned that we give, but how we give. He is looking for those who give joyfully, willingly, and in faith. Giving shouldn't feel like a burden—it should be an act of worship and an expression of gratitude.

1. **God LOVES a cheerful giver** – When we give with a joyful heart, we are aligning ourselves with the heart of God. Who doesn't want to be the kind of giver that God loves to see?
2. **Cheerful giving is an act of faith** – It declares, *"God, I trust You as my provider."* True faith isn't fearful in giving—it finds joy in sowing.
3. **A cheerful giver is also a cheerful receiver** – When we give with joy, we also reap with joy! God doesn't just supply—He blesses abundantly, filling our lives with more than enough.

The Joy of Generosity

- Giving isn't about loss; it's about **gain**—not just financially, but in God's favor, provision, and supernatural supply.
- The world sees giving as **losing something**—but the Kingdom sees it as sowing something.
- Our giving should be **full of faith, excitement, and expectation**—because we know that God is faithful to His Word.

Make the Choice to Be a Cheerful Giver

We all get to choose our attitude toward giving. We can give reluctantly, or we can give cheerfully, knowing that God loves it! If God loves a cheerful giver, then we should make sure we are the kind of giver He loves to see!

PowerPoint:

If God LOVES a 'cheerful' giver... then that's the kind of giver I'm going to make sure I am!

18.

Delighting in Obeying His Word

Scripture: Psalm 112:1–3 (ESV)

"Praise the Lord! Blessed is the man who fears the Lord,
who greatly delights in His commandments!
His offspring will be mighty in the land;
the generation of the upright will be blessed.
Wealth and riches are in his house,
and his righteousness endures forever."

The Blessing of Obedience

Obedience to God's Word is not a **burden**—it's a **delight**! The Bible teaches that those who love and obey His commands will experience supernatural blessings. Many people want the promises of God, but they forget that most of God's promises have conditions.

God's Promise and Its Condition

In this passage, God lays out **three incredible blessings** for those who delight in His commandments:

1. **Your offspring will be mighty in the land** – Obedience doesn't just bless you—it impacts your children and future generations.

2. **Wealth and riches will be in your house** – Financial blessing follows those who live according to God's principles.
3. **Your righteousness will endure forever** – Walking in obedience establishes a lasting legacy of faith.

But notice the condition: *"Who greatly delights in his commandments."* God's blessings are attached to our willingness and joy in following His ways.

Obedience Positions Us for Overflow

Many people ask God to bless them, but they overlook the clear instruction He has already given. When it comes to tithes and offerings, God doesn't just suggest it—He commands it. Malachi 3:10 says that when we bring the tithe into His house, **He will open the windows of heaven over our lives.**

Obedience in Giving Unlocks God's Best

- We don't give out of obligation—we give because we trust God's Word.
- God doesn't bless hesitant, reluctant obedience—He blesses those who delight in His commands.
- True faith is joyful obedience, knowing that God is faithful to fulfill His Word.

PowerPoint:

When we obey God's Word, we receive His promise! He says to bring the tithes and offerings into His house, and He will open the windows of heaven over your life and bless you to overflowing!

19.

The Measure of Overflow

Scripture: Mark 4:24

"Then He said to them, 'Take heed what you hear. With the same measure you use, it will be measured to you; and to you who hear, more will be given.'"

Scripture: 2 Corinthians 9:6

"But this I say: He who sows sparingly will also reap sparingly, and he who sows bountifully will also reap bountifully."

Living in the Overflow

God's Kingdom operates on the principle of measure—we determine how much we receive by how much we are willing to give. Many people pray for increase, provision, and abundance, but the reality is that God's level of blessing in our lives is connected to our level of giving and faith.

Choosing the Measure of Your Blessing

- **Your level of giving determines your level of receiving** – If you sow sparingly, you will reap sparingly. If you sow bountifully, you will reap bountifully.

- **Faith plays a role in overflow** – Jesus said the measure we use is the measure that will be used for us. If we believe for small, we receive small. If we believe for abundance, we position ourselves for abundance.
- **We can't expect a great harvest with a small seed** – Farmers understand this principle. You can't plant a tiny amount and expect a huge return. The greater the seed, the greater the harvest.

We Choose the Measure of Our Overflow

- Some people give and believe in small measure, like using a spoon.
- Others step up their faith and give generously, like using a cup.
- But those who truly trust God's principles and live generously give with a bucket, expecting overflow!

God isn't **holding back blessing—He responds to our measure!** If we want to see overflowing provision, supernatural abundance, and increase, we must step out in faith and give accordingly.

PowerPoint:

The measure we use determines the measure we receive. We can choose to use a spoon, a cup, or a bucket!

20.

The Attitude for Harvest

Scripture: 2 Corinthians 9:6-7 (NLT)

"Remember this—a farmer who plants only a few seeds will get a small crop. But the one who plants generously will get a generous crop. You must each decide in your heart how much to give. And don't give reluctantly or in response to pressure. 'For God loves a person who gives cheerfully.'"

The Principle of Sowing and Reaping

Every farmer understands this: **The size of the harvest is determined by the amount of seed sown.** The same is true in God's Kingdom. Giving is sowing, and sowing always leads to harvest.

1. **We sow into the Kingdom, knowing that our giving results in a harvest of souls.**
   - Every time we give, we are making an eternal investment.
   - Our giving enables the gospel to be preached, churches to be built, and lives to be transformed.
   - The more we sow, the more souls are won into the Kingdom.

2. **Our attitude matters in giving.**
   - God isn't just looking at the amount we give—He's looking at the heart behind it.
   - Giving should never be done reluctantly or under pressure.
   - Cheerful giving is faith-filled giving—it's an act of trust that God is our provider and rewarder.

Giving Positions Us for a Personal Harvest

Not only does our giving bring a harvest in the Kingdom, but also it also positions us for God's blessing.

- God is faithful to **pour back into the lives** of those who give with the right heart.
- When we give **joyfully and generously**, we align ourselves with His economy of supernatural provision.
- A stingy heart leads to small results, but a faith-filled, joyful giver reaps abundantly.

An Attitude of Faith and Joy Brings Great Reward

Our mindset toward giving will **determine our level of harvest.** If we give with **doubt and reluctance,** we limit what God can do. But when we give with expectation, joy, and faith, we open the door for God's abundant blessings to flow.

PowerPoint:

An attitude of faith (our giving results in souls) and joy brings a great reward!

21.

God Is My Master

Scripture: Matthew 6:24

"No one can serve two masters; for either he will hate the one and love the other, or else he will be loyal to the one and despise the other. You cannot serve God and mammon."

The Choice of Mastery

Jesus makes it clear—**we can't serve both God and money**. Money itself is not evil, but when it becomes our master, it competes for the place that only God should have in our lives.

Stewardship Is a Heart Issue

- Stewardship is about managing everything we have—our time, resources, finances, and even our gifts.
- God doesn't need our money—He wants our hearts.
- Giving is not about God's financial needs, but about our relationship with Him.

Obedience in Tithes and Offerings

- As believers, we are called to obey in the area of tithing and offerings.

- Tithing is not about losing money—it's about trusting God as our provider and master.
- If God doesn't have our money, He doesn't fully have our heart.

Where Is Your Treasure?

Matthew 6:21 reminds us: *"For where your treasure is, there your heart will be also."*

- What we invest in reveals what we value most.
- If we want our hearts to be fully aligned with God's will, we must surrender every area, including our finances.
- True freedom comes when we let God, not money, rule our lives.

PowerPoint:

God knows if He doesn't have our money, then He doesn't have our heart. Where our treasure is, that's where our heart will be also.

22.

The Love of Money

Scripture: 1 Timothy 6:10

"For the love of money is a root of all kinds of evil, for which some have strayed from the faith in their greediness and pierced themselves through with many sorrows."

Money Is Not the Problem—The Love of Money Is

One of the most **misquoted verses** in the Bible is **"money is the root of all evil."** That's not what Scripture actually says. Money itself is neutral—it can be used for good or for evil. The problem is the love of money—when money takes the place in our hearts that belongs to God.

- Money is a tool—it is neither righteous nor sinful.
- The love of money leads to deception—it pulls people away from faith and into greed.
- We are called to love God and use money, not the other way around.

What Do You Love?

Money is a great **servant**, but a terrible master.

- When money controls a person, it leads to greed, compromise, and destruction.
- When God is our master, money becomes a powerful tool for the Kingdom.
- We love God, but we use money—to reach the lost, build churches, and bless others.

Money's Kingdom Purpose

Money in itself isn't evil—it's how we handle it that determines its impact.

- Money says YES to building churches, sending missionaries, feeding the poor, and spreading the gospel.
- We don't worship money, we steward it—we direct it toward God's purposes.
- We must guard our hearts so that we trust in God, not in wealth.

PowerPoint:

Money says YES to reaching the lost, building churches, and feeding the poor. Money is not evil, but WHAT/WHO we love determines how we use it.

23.

Acknowledging God's Ownership

Scripture: 1 Timothy 6:17–19 (NLT)

"Teach those who are rich in this world not to be proud and not to trust in their money, which is so unreliable. Their trust should be in God, who richly gives us all we need for our enjoyment. Tell them to use their money to do good. They should be rich in good works and generous to those in need, always being ready to share with others. By doing this, they will be storing up their treasure as a good foundation for the future so that they may experience true life."

The Principle of Stewardship

The Bible teaches us that **we own nothing—God owns it all.** Stewardship isn't just about handling money wisely; it's about acknowledging that everything we have belongs to God.

- **We are not owners, we are managers.** Everything in our hands—our money, time, and talents—belongs to the Lord.
- **Trust must be in God, not wealth.** Money is uncertain, but God's provision is unfailing.

- **The priority of stewardship** is to use what we have for His purposes, not just for personal gain.

Faithfulness Leads to Greater Blessing

When we handle what God has given us with obedience and generosity, He entrusts us with more. The Bible speaks of true riches, which are Kingdom resources, influence, and greater opportunities to impact lives.

- A faithful steward is one who understands that their resources are a tool for God's glory.
- Those who use their money to do good are storing up treasure in heaven.
- Stewardship is not just about giving but about aligning our resources with God's will.

The Lordship of Christ over Our Resources

Acknowledging God's ownership means we **honor Him first.** This is why we bring the tithe to His house—because it already belongs to Him. When we give, we are not losing; we are demonstrating trust in God's provision and aligning with His Kingdom economy.

PowerPoint:

Everything we have belongs to the Lord, and we acknowledge His lordship over it. Therefore, as good stewards, we bring to His house what belongs to Him.

24.

Blessed to Be a Blessing

Scripture: Genesis 12:2

"I will make you a great nation; I will bless you and make your name great; and you shall be a blessing."

God's Blessing Has a Purpose

The call of God upon Abraham's life serves as a model for all believers. God's promise to bless Abraham was not just for his own benefit but so that he could **be a blessing to others.**

- **God's blessing is never meant to stop with us**—it is designed to flow through us.
- **He blesses us so that we can bring impact**—to our families, our communities, and even the nations.
- The **Kingdom mindset** isn't just about what we receive, but about what we release.

Abundance for Every Good Work

"And God is able to make all grace abound toward you, that you, always having all sufficiency in all things, may have an abundance for every good work.

2 Corinthians 9:8

- God's blessing in our lives is **not random**—it is for the purpose of **advancing His Kingdom.**
- He supplies **more than enough** so that we are always ready to give, serve, and impact.
- We are called to **live in overflow**, not just for ourselves, but to bless the world around us.

Biblical Stewardship: A Kingdom Assignment

Stewardship is not just about sustaining the church—it's about **fulfilling our divine purpose.** We are blessed so that we can be conduits of God's provision to:

- support the work of the gospel,
- build the local church,
- meet the needs of the poor,
- impact the nations with generosity.

PowerPoint:

The purpose of biblical stewardship is not just so that the church can function, but IT IS IN OUR GOD-GIVEN DNA TO BE A BLESSING TO THE NATIONS!

25.

Finding Our Treasure

Scripture: Matthew 6:19–21

"Do not lay up for yourselves treasures on earth, where moth and rust destroy and where thieves break in and steal; but lay up for yourselves treasures in heaven, where neither moth nor rust destroys and where thieves do not break in and steal. For where your treasure is, there your heart will be also."

God Wants Our Heart

God is not against us having things—He is against things having us. He wants our hearts fully surrendered to Him, and He knows that one of the biggest competitors for our hearts is money and material possessions.

- **The only thing of value we can truly give God is our heart**—and that is what He desires most.
- **If our heart is tangled up in possessions, status, and wealth,** it's difficult for God to have full access to our lives.
- Jesus makes it clear: Our hearts don't determine where our treasure goes—**our treasure determines where our heart follows.**

The Heart Follows the Treasure

Many people believe that when their heart is in the right place, they will start giving. But **Jesus flips that thinking**—He says that our giving actually leads our heart.

- If we want to be more passionate about God's Kingdom, we must invest in it.
- If we want our heart to be fully devoted to God, we must put our treasure in His hands.
- When we bring our treasure into the Kingdom, our heart naturally follows.

How to Store Up Treasure in Heaven

We lay up treasures in heaven by:

1. Giving generously to God's work.
2. Sowing into the local church, missions, and Kingdom initiatives.
3. Prioritizing eternal investments over temporary wealth.

The more we invest in the Kingdom, the more our heart aligns with God's mission.

PowerPoint:

"Where our treasure IS, our heart WILL BE ALSO... NOT vice versa!"

26.

Giving Is a Matter of Trust

Scripture: Luke 16:10-11

"He who is faithful in what is least is faithful also in much; and he who is unjust in what is least is unjust also in much. Therefore, if you have not been faithful in the unrighteous mammon, who will commit to your trust the true riches?"

The Test of Stewardship

Giving is not just about money—it is a **test of trust.** Jesus makes it clear in this passage that money is the least of all things, yet how we handle it determines whether we can be trusted with true riches.

- Money is temporary, but God's Kingdom is eternal.
- Faithfulness in finances reflects faithfulness in greater responsibilities.
- If we mishandle earthly wealth, how can God entrust us with spiritual influence, divine revelation, and greater Kingdom assignments?

The Principle of Trust and Increase

Many people ask God for **greater blessings, more responsibility, and increased anointing**, but Jesus makes it clear: faithfulness in small things opens the door for bigger things.

- **Money is a test**—how we manage it determines how much God can entrust us with.
- If we are **generous and faithful in giving**, God knows we are ready for greater things.
- The **true riches** are not material possessions but spiritual authority, Kingdom influence, and divine opportunities.

Testing God in Giving

Malachi 3:10 is the only place in the Bible where God invites us to test Him:

"Bring all the tithes into the storehouse ... and try Me now in this," says the Lord of hosts, "if I will not open for you the windows of heaven and pour out for you such blessing that there will not be room enough to receive it."

- God challenges us to trust Him—to test Him in our giving and see His faithfulness.
- This principle is repeated throughout Scripture: when we give, we position ourselves for supernatural provision and increase.

PowerPoint:

Money is simply a test for the greater things that God wants to do in our lives. That's why in Malachi, the Lord actually tells us to 'test Him' in giving and see what He will do!

27.

The Battle for Lordship

Scripture: Matthew 6:24

"No one can serve two masters; for either
he will hate the one and love the other,
or else he will be loyal to the one and despise the other.
You cannot serve God and mammon."

Jesus is clear—**we can't serve two masters.** The real question is not whether we will serve, but who we will serve. Money and material wealth try to claim our loyalty, but God calls us to trust Him as our provider.

- **Money is a tool, not a master** – It's meant to serve us, not rule us.
- **Mammon represents a system of dependence on wealth rather than God** – It competes for our heart, demanding control over our decisions and priorities.
- **The issue is trust** – Where do we place our trust: God's promises or financial security?

Stewardship Reflects Our Master

Being a faithful steward means recognizing that everything we have belongs to God.

- Tithing and giving are not just about obligation—they are about lordship.
- God doesn't need our money—He desires our full trust and devotion.
- When we give freely and joyfully, we declare: *"God, You are my provider and master, not my money."*

Trusting God Over Mammon

Many people hesitate to release their finances because they fear lack. But trusting God means we believe He is our source, not just for today but for our future.

- **Faith says:** "I put God first, and He will take care of the rest."
- **Fear says:** "I need to hold on, just in case."
- **Giving tests our allegiance** – It reveals whether we trust God's Kingdom economy or the world's system.

The Blessing of Serving God First

- When we put God first, He releases abundance, favor, and provision.
- When we hold back, we limit what He wants to do in our lives.
- True financial freedom comes when we let God, not money, dictate our lives.

PowerPoint:

If God doesn't have our money, He doesn't have our heart. Where our treasure is, that's where our heart will be also.

28.

Not Equal Giving, But Equal Sacrifice

Scripture: Luke 21:1–4

"And He looked up and saw the rich putting their gifts into the treasury, and He saw also a certain poor widow putting in two mites. So He said, 'Truly I say to you that this poor widow has put in more than all; for all these out of their abundance have put in offerings for God, but she out of her poverty put in all the livelihood that she had.'"

The Heart of Giving: Open Hand, Willing Heart

Throughout Scripture, God doesn't measure giving by the amount but by the heart and sacrifice behind it.

- God is not looking for equal amounts—He's looking for equal sacrifice.
- Giving should move us—because when it moves us, it moves God.
- The widow's two mites had greater value in the Kingdom than the large sums given out of abundance—because she gave sacrificially.

The Principle of Sacrificial Giving

1. **God sees the heart, not the amount.** The rich gave what was comfortable; the widow gave what cost her something.
2. **Sacrifice demonstrates faith.** When we give beyond what is easy, we step into a place of trusting God as our provider.
3. **A heart of sacrifice attracts divine attention.** Jesus didn't stop to commend the large givers—He highlighted the widow's faith and sacrifice.

Giving that Moves God

- Giving should not be about duty, but about faith and worship.
- When we give sacrificially, we are aligning ourselves with God's supernatural provision.
- The seed that leaves your hand never leaves your life—it goes into your future and produces a harvest.

PowerPoint:

Let's give with an open hand and a willing heart as we bring the Lord's tithe and give offerings over and above. REMEMBER: When we give to God in faith—the seed that leaves your hand, never leaves your life!

29.

Kingdom Culture and an Abundance Mindset

Scripture: 2 Corinthians 9:8 (RSV)

"And God is able to provide you with every blessing in abundance, so that you may always have enough of everything and may provide in abundance for every good work."

Kingdom Culture Is Built on Generosity

The culture of God's Kingdom operates on an abundance mindset—not lack, not scarcity, but overflow. Why? Because the **King of this Kingdom is El Shaddai—the God who is more than enough!** He is Jehovah Jireh—the Lord our Provider!

- In God's Kingdom, we don't fear running out—we trust in the Source who never runs dry.
- Kingdom thinking is not about just having enough, but also having more than enough—to be a blessing.
- When we live generously, we reflect the heart of our generous King!

Abundance Has a Purpose

Paul tells us that God blesses us, **not just for personal provision**, but so we can fund every good work.

- If God can get it through me, He will get it to me.
- When we live with an open hand, we become a channel for God's blessing to flow to others.
- If we release what's in our hand, God releases what's in His hand—and His hand is far greater than ours!

We Are Channels of God's Grace and Provision

The world teaches people to hold on tightly to what they have. But Kingdom people **live with open hands—sowing, blessing, and trusting that God will provide even more.**

- When we sow, we activate the cycle of Kingdom increase.
- We are blessed to be a blessing.
- Our giving doesn't just meet needs—it multiplies, bringing impact beyond what we can imagine!

PowerPoint:

God will always provide everything we need—not only for us but so that we can be a blessing!

30.

God's Supply Never Runs Out

Scripture: Philippians 4:19

"And my God shall supply all your need according to His riches in glory by Christ Jesus."

God Is Our Source, Not the World

Many people operate with a scarcity mindset, believing that resources are limited, but in God's economy, there is no lack! He is El Shaddai—the God of more than enough. When we live according to Kingdom principles, we don't have to worry about running out because we serve a God whose supply never runs dry.

- The world says: "Hold on tight—you never know what will happen!"
- The Kingdom says: "Give, and it will be given to you!"
- The world operates on fear, but the Kingdom operates on faith.

God's Provision Is Unlimited

Paul reminds us in Philippians 4:19 that God's supply isn't based on the world's economy, our bank accounts, or our jobs—it's based on His riches in glory! That means:

- God's resources are never depleted – Heaven is not running out!
- His provision is not based on natural circumstances – Even in famine, God provides for His people.
- He supplies ALL our needs, not just some of them!

Provision Is Connected to Obedience

Before Paul declared *"God shall supply all your need,"* he was speaking to givers—people who had been generous in supporting the work of the ministry.

- Provision follows obedience.
- Giving positions us for divine supply.
- When we trust God with our finances, we step into a supernatural economy.

God's Economy Never Fails

- Inflation doesn't affect God.
- Recessions don't affect God.
- Shortages don't affect God.

He is still Jehovah Jireh—the Lord who provides!

The Key to Living in Overflow

- Trust God as your provider, not your paycheck.
- Be obedient in tithing and giving.

- Sow generously, expecting God's supernatural supply.

PowerPoint:

God is our source, and His supply never runs out!

31.

The Law of Seedtime and Harvest

Scripture: Genesis 8:22

> *"While the earth remains, seedtime and harvest,*
> *cold and heat, winter and summer,*
> *and day and night shall not cease."*

The Principle of Sowing and Reaping

God has established a spiritual law that governs increase—it's called **seedtime and harvest.** Just like in the natural world, when a farmer plants a seed, a harvest will come. **This is not just a financial principle; it's a Kingdom law that applies to every area of life.**

- Every harvest begins with a seed.
- What we plant determines what we will reap.
- We don't reap immediately, but in due season, the harvest comes!

Your Seed Determines Your Future

Many people expect a harvest but have never planted a seed. We wouldn't go to a field and expect crops to appear without planting anything—so why do we expect God to bless us financially if we have never sown into His Kingdom?

- If we sow love, we reap love.
- If we sow kindness, we reap kindness.
- If we sow finances, we reap financial blessing.

Paul reinforces this in 2 Corinthians 9:6:

"He who sows sparingly will also reap sparingly, and he who sows bountifully will also reap bountifully."

The measure of our sowing determines the measure of our reaping.

Faith Is Required in Sowing

A farmer doesn't plant a seed and then dig it up the next day to see if it's working—he trusts the process. Giving requires faith:

- Faith that God will multiply what we sow.
- Faith that our seed will produce in due time.
- Faith that God's economy is not subject to earthly conditions.

Seed Leaves Your Hand, But Never Your Life

When we give, we are not **losing** something—we are **planting** something that will produce a supernatural return.

- The seed may leave our hand, but it doesn't leave our future.
- God takes what we sow and multiplies it in ways we cannot imagine.

- A seed always produces a greater harvest than what was sown!

Sowing into Good Ground

Not every place is good ground, but the **Kingdom of God is the best soil for our financial seed.** When we bring the tithe, give offerings, and sow into the work of the gospel, we are ensuring that our seed produces an eternal impact.

PowerPoint:

We don't lose when we give—we plant, and God brings the increase!

32.

God Multiplies What We Give

Scripture: Luke 6:38

"Give, and it will be given to you: good measure, pressed down, shaken together, and running over will be put into your bosom. For with the same measure that you use, it will be measured back to you."

Giving Is Not Subtraction—It's Multiplication

One of the greatest Kingdom principles is that **God never asks us to give so that we have less—He asks us to give so He can multiply what we have!**

- In the natural world , giving decreases what we possess.
- In the Kingdom, giving increases what we possess!
- When we release what's in our hand, God releases what's in His hand—and His hand is much bigger!

God's System of Increase

In Luke 6:38, Jesus teaches us that the measure we use determines the measure we receive.

- **Good measure** – God gives back in abundance.

- **Pressed down** – He makes room for more.
- **Shaken together** – He removes limitations.
- **Running over** – He doesn't just add—He overflows!

God's Multiplication Principle

When Jesus fed the 5,000+, the miracle of multiplication didn't happen until the little was released into His hands. A small boy gave five loaves and two fish, and Jesus blessed and multiplied it until everyone was fed—with twelve baskets left over!

- Multiplication happens in God's hands, not in ours.
- What we give, God multiplies—exceedingly and abundantly!
- Giving in faith creates room for supernatural increase.

The Faith Factor in Giving

- **Fear says,** "I can't afford to give."
- **Faith says,** "I can't afford not to give!"
- **Fear holds back, but faith releases**—and faith is what pleases God.

Sowing with Expectation

When a farmer plants seed, he doesn't wonder if something will grow—he expects it. We must sow with that same expectation—knowing that God is faithful to bring a harvest.

- We don't give to get, but we understand that giving positions us to receive.
- God is not looking for a way to take from us—He's looking for a way to bless us!

PowerPoint:

What we give, God multiplies back in abundance!

33.

What's in Your Hand?

Scripture: Exodus 4:2

So the Lord said to him, 'What is that in your hand?' He said, 'A rod.'

God Uses What We Already Have

When God called Moses to lead Israel out of Egypt, Moses felt unqualified and insufficient for the task. But God didn't ask Moses for something he didn't have—He asked him to use what was already in his hand.

- Moses saw a **simple staff**—God saw a tool for miracles.
- Moses saw **his limitation**—God saw unlimited potential.
- Moses saw **his weakness**—God saw His power working through him.

This is how God works in our giving! He isn't asking us to give what we don't have—He's asking us to release what is already in our hands.

What We Release, God Uses for His Glory

- The widow in 1 Kings 17 had only a little oil and flour, but when she gave it in faith, God multiplied her supply.
- The little boy in John 6 had only five loaves and two fish, but when he gave it to Jesus, it fed thousands.
- God never asks for what we don't have—He asks us to trust Him with what we do have.

Giving Activates the Miraculous

Many people wait for a financial breakthrough before they give, but Kingdom thinking is different. Breakthrough follows obedience!

- **Fear says,** "I don't have enough."
- **Faith says,** "What I have is enough for God to use."
- When we give what's in our hand, we unlock what's in God's hand!

Your Giving Is a Seed for Your Future

- A farmer doesn't wait for a full harvest to plant a seed—he plants first, knowing a harvest is coming.
- The same is true in our finances: When we sow, we activate a Kingdom principle that leads to increase.

- Nothing multiplies until it is released!

PowerPoint:

"God uses what we give to accomplish miracles!"

34.

Breaking the Spirit of Mammon

Scripture: Matthew 6:24

"You cannot serve God and mammon."

Money Is a Tool, Not a Master

Jesus made it clear—**money is not just currency; it has a spirit behind it.** Mammon represents a worldly system of wealth, greed, and self-reliance that competes for our trust and allegiance.

- Mammon wants our worship. It wants us to trust money over God.
- God wants our hearts. He calls us to trust Him as our provider.
- The issue is not money itself, but whether money controls us.

Tithing and Generosity Break Mammon's Hold

When we tithe and give, we are making a bold declaration:

- *"Money is not my master—God is!"*
- *"I don't serve wealth—I serve the One who provides it."*

- *"My trust is not in my paycheck—it's in my Provider!"*

Giving breaks fear, greed, and self-reliance! When we bring our finances under God's authority, we step into His supernatural economy.

Many people hesitate to give because they feel like they can't afford it. But God's economy works differently:

- **The world says:** Hold on to everything you have.
- **God says:** Release what's in your hand, and I will release what's in Mine.
- **The world says:** You can't afford to give.
- **God says:** You can't afford not to give!

Kingdom Living Requires a Shift in Thinking

1. Money is a terrible master but a great servant.
2. We don't serve money—we use it for Kingdom purposes.
3. Breaking mammon's hold allows us to live in freedom and blessing.

The Power of Surrendered Finances

When we put **God first** in our finances, we experience:

Freedom from financial fear.

Supernatural provision and increase.

A heart aligned with God's purposes.

PowerPoint:

When we trust God with our finances, we declare He is our provider!

35.

You Can't Outgive God

Scripture: 2 Corinthians 9:10 (NLT)

"For God is the one who provides seed for the farmer and then bread to eat. In the same way, He will provide and increase your resources and then produce a great harvest of generosity in you."

God Is the Source of Every Blessing

Everything we have comes from God—He is the One who provides both seed to sow and bread to eat. That means:

- God gives us the resources we need.
- He increases what we release in faith.
- He brings a harvest so we can continue the cycle of generosity.

Giving Is a Cycle, Not a One-Time Event

Some people hesitate to give because they fear losing what they have. But in God's economy, **giving is never loss—it's investment into something greater.**

- A farmer doesn't hesitate to plant seed—he knows it will produce a harvest.

- The more we sow, the greater our harvest.
- God supplies, we sow, and He multiplies!

The Kingdom Principle of Multiplication

Jesus demonstrated this principle when He fed the 5,000+:

- A boy gave five loaves and two fish, which seemed insignificant.
- Jesus blessed it, multiplied it, and thousands were fed—with twelve baskets left over!

What we release into God's hands, He always multiplies beyond what we expect.

Overflow Is God's Design

Luke 6:38 says: "*Give, and it will be given to you: good measure, pressed down, shaken together, and running over will be put into your bosom.*"

- Giving doesn't deplete us—it positions us for supernatural increase.
- We don't give to lose—we give to receive so we can keep on giving.
- God's Kingdom is built on overflow, not scarcity!

The Challenge: Test God in This!

- If we trust Him and release what's in our hand, He will release what's in His.
- We will always see greater provision, greater blessing, and greater opportunities to give again.

- We can't outgive God—He always outgives us!

PowerPoint:

When we give, God always outgives us in return!

36.

The Anointing for Increase

Scripture: Deuteronomy 8:18

"And you shall remember the Lord your God,
for it is He who gives you power to get wealth,
that He may establish His covenant which
He swore to your fathers, as it is this day."

God Gives Us the Power to Prosper

Many people think of wealth as something that comes from hard work, skill, or luck, but Scripture is clear—it is God who gives us the power to create wealth.

- Wealth is not just about money—it's about abundance, provision, and influence.
- The ability to increase is not a worldly idea—it's a Kingdom principle!
- God doesn't just want to bless us—He wants to establish His covenant through us.

Prosperity with a Purpose

God doesn't bless us just so we can accumulate wealth—He blesses us so we can advance His Kingdom!

- If God can get it through us, He will get it to us.
- The more we give, the more we position ourselves for supernatural increase.
- The blessing of God is not about greed—it's about impact!

Wealth Is a Tool for Kingdom Expansion

Some people struggle with the idea of wealth in the church, but the truth is, the more resources we have, the more we can do for the gospel!

- Churches are built, missionaries are sent, the hungry are fed—all because of Kingdom generosity.
- God is looking for people He can trust with increase—people who will use it for His purposes.
- A poverty mindset limits what God wants to do—but a Kingdom mindset releases the anointing for abundance.

Break Free from a Scarcity Mentality

The enemy wants believers to live in lack and fear, thinking that prosperity is for someone else. But the Bible says:

- "The blessing of the Lord makes one rich, and He adds no sorrow with it." (Proverbs 10:22)
- "Seek first the Kingdom of God... and all these things shall be added to you." (Matthew 6:33)

- "God is able to make all grace abound toward you… having all sufficiency in all things." (2 Corinthians 9:8)

When we trust God and operate in a spirit of generosity, we step into the anointing for increase!

PowerPoint:

God gives us the anointing for increase so we can advance His Kingdom!

37.

God Provides Before We Need It

Scripture: Genesis 22:14

And Abraham called the name of the place,
The-Lord-Will-Provide; as it is said to this day,
'In the Mount of the Lord it shall be provided.'

Jehovah Jireh—The Lord Who Provides

One of the greatest revelations in Scripture is that God provides before we even recognize the need. When Abraham was on the mountain about to sacrifice Isaac, God had already prepared a ram in the thicket.

- Abraham didn't see the provision at first, but God had already placed it there.
- Provision is often waiting on the other side of our obedience.
- God is never late—He is always working behind the scenes to supply what we need.

Faith Positions Us for Supernatural Supply

- Abraham trusted God's provision even when he didn't see it yet.

- Many times, we hesitate to give because we focus on what we don't have instead of who our Provider is.
- When we trust God with our giving, we are declaring: "*God, You are my source—not my job, not the economy, not my bank account!*"

God Sees the Need Before We Do

- **The ram was already in place** before Abraham got to the mountain.
- **The fish with the coin was already in the sea** before Peter needed to pay the temple tax.
- **The loaves and fish were already in the crowd** before Jesus needed to feed the 5,000.

The same is true in our lives—before we even recognize a financial need, God has already prepared the supply!

Obedience Unlocks Provision

- Abraham had to step in faith before he saw the ram.
- Peter had to cast his net before he caught the fish with the coin.
- The boy had to release his lunch before Jesus multiplied it.

When we **tithe, give, and sow generously,** we are walking in the same faith—trusting that God has already made a way!

PowerPoint:

"Before we even recognize a need, God has already provided the supply!"

38.

Sowing in Famine Brings Supernatural Harvest

Scripture: Genesis 26:12

"Then Isaac sowed in that land,
and reaped in the same year a hundredfold;
and the Lord blessed him."

Faith Moves in the Opposite Spirit

Isaac lived in a time of **famine**, a season when the natural world said: "Hold on to what you have. Don't take risks. Now is not the time to sow." But Isaac did something radical—he sowed anyway.

- **The world says,** *"It's a bad time to give."*
- **Faith says:** *"Now is the time to trust God more than ever!"*
- Isaac didn't let his circumstances dictate his giving—he let his faith in God's provision lead him.

God's Economy Is Not Limited by Earth's Conditions

The Bible says **Isaac reaped a hundredfold in the same year!** How is that possible during a famine?

Because:

- God honors faith-filled obedience.
- Sowing in difficult seasons positions us for supernatural return.
- God's ability to bless is never dictated by natural circumstances.

When We Give in Faith, We Position Ourselves for Increase

- Some people wait for abundance before they give—but that's not how Kingdom economy works!
- Isaac sowed before he saw the harvest.
- When we give, we activate the supernatural principle of increase.

The Principle of Sowing in Tough Times

This principle is repeated throughout Scripture:

- The widow of Zarephath gave her last meal to Elijah in the middle of a famine—and God supernaturally multiplied her supply (1 Kings 17:8-16).
- The disciples gave Jesus five loaves and two fish when there wasn't enough food—and He multiplied it to feed thousands (John 6:9-13).
- When we give in faith, even when it seems inconvenient, God shows up in supernatural ways!

God's Promise for Those Who Trust Him

Psalm 37:19 (NIV) says:

"In times of disaster they will not wither; in days of famine they will enjoy plenty."

- When the world is struggling, God's people will flourish.
- Sowing in faith leads to reaping in abundance.
- We are part of a Kingdom that is never in recession!

PowerPoint:

Famine says hold back—faith says sow! When we give in faith, we position ourselves for supernatural increase!

39.

Giving Makes Room for More

Scripture: Proverbs 11:24

"There is one who scatters, yet increases more;
and there is one who withholds more than is right,
but it leads to poverty."

The Kingdom Principle of Expansion

Naturally, we think that the more we hold onto, the more we will have. But in God's Kingdom, the opposite is true—the more we release, the more He increases us.

- Generosity creates capacity for God to bless us.
- Withholding leads to limitation and lack.
- When we trust God with what we have, He entrusts us with more.

The World vs. The Kingdom

- **The world says:** *"Hold tightly to what you have."*
- **The Kingdom says:** *"Sow generously, and God will multiply it."*
- **The world says:** *"Giving makes you have less."*
- **The Kingdom says:** *"Giving makes room for increase."*

The truth is: A closed hand can't receive, but an open hand is positioned for overflow!

Why Some People Feel Stuck Financially

Many people struggle financially, not because they don't have enough, but because they haven't activated the principle of generosity.

- We can't expect a harvest if we never plant a seed.
- God blesses faithful stewards who live with an open hand.
- Giving is a supernatural act that invites supernatural provision.

Examples of Increase Through Generosity

- Abraham was willing to give up Isaac in faith, and God not only provided but also made him the father of nations (Genesis 22:16-17).
- The early church lived in radical generosity, and as a result, there was no lack among them (Acts 4:34-35).
- Solomon, after offering extravagant sacrifices, received supernatural wisdom and wealth beyond measure (1 Kings 3:4-13).

The Promise of Overflow

Luke 6:38:

"Give, and it will be given to you: good measure, pressed down, shaken together, and running over will be put into your bosom."

- God is a God of abundance, not lack.
- When we pour out, He pours in.
- Living with an open hand ensures we are never empty!

PowerPoint:

A closed hand can't receive, but an open hand makes room for more!

40.

Faith Is Released in Giving

Scripture: Hebrews 11:6

"But without faith it is impossible to please Him, for he who comes to God must believe that He is, and that He is a rewarder of those who diligently seek Him."

Giving Is an Act of Faith

Every time we give, we are exercising faith. Giving isn't just a financial transaction—it's a **spiritual declaration that we trust God as our source and provider.**

- Faith isn't just believing—faith is action.
- Giving is proof that we trust God to take care of us.
- Every time we give, we are saying, "God, You are my provider, and I believe You will supply all my needs."

Faith-Filled Giving Breaks Fear

Many people hesitate to give because of fear—fear of not having enough, fear of unexpected bills, fear of lack. But faith-filled giving breaks the spirit of fear and releases supernatural provision.

- **Fear says,** *"What if I don't have enough?"*

- **Faith says,** *"God is my source, and He will provide more than enough!"*
- Fear holds back, but faith steps forward!

Giving Requires Believing Before Seeing

Hebrews 11:1 says:

"Now faith is the substance of things hoped for, the evidence of things not seen."

- A farmer doesn't wait for a full harvest before he plants seed—he sows in faith, knowing the harvest will come.
- When we give, we don't give based on what we have—we give based on who God is.
- We don't wait for overflow to start giving—our giving brings the overflow!

God Rewards Faithful Givers

The second half of Hebrews 11:6 says that God is a rewarder of those who diligently seek Him.

- God never ignores acts of faith.
- When we give in faith, we set ourselves up for supernatural blessings.
- The size of our faith determines the size of our harvest!

Examples of Faith-Filled Giving

- **Abraham tithed before the law was even given (Genesis 14:20)**—he wasn't commanded, but he gave in faith and became the father of nations.
- **Hannah gave her firstborn son Samuel to the Lord (1 Samuel 1:27-28)**—she released what was most precious to her, and God blessed her with many more children.
- **The poor widow gave two mites (Luke 21:1-4)**—Jesus said she gave more than anyone because she gave out of faith, not surplus.

Faith-Filled Giving Positions Us for Supernatural Increase

Faith-filled giving is **not about losing—it's about positioning ourselves for increase.** When we give, we open the door for:

Divine provision

Supernatural opportunities

Overflow and abundance

PowerPoint:

"Giving isn't just about money—it's about faith! Fear holds back, but faith releases blessing!"

41.

Tithing Is a Covenant Connection

Scripture: Leviticus 27:30

"And all the tithe of the land, whether of the seed of the land or of the fruit of the tree, is the LORD's. It is holy to the LORD."

The Tithe Belongs to the Lord

Tithing is not just an **Old Testament practice**—it is a **Kingdom principle** that connects us to God's covenant of provision. The Bible is clear: The tithe already belongs to God.

- We don't "give" the tithe—we return it.
- Tithing is not a donation—it's an act of obedience.
- When we honor God with the tithe, we acknowledge Him as our source and provider.

Tithing Keeps Us in Covenant Blessing

Malachi 3:10 tells us:

"Bring all the tithes into the storehouse, that there may be food in My house, and try Me now in this," says the Lord of hosts, "if I will not open for you the windows of heaven and pour out for you such blessing that there will not be room enough to receive it."

- Tithing keeps us in position to receive supernatural provision.
- God promises to open the windows of heaven when we honor Him first.
- Tithing isn't about legalism—it's about trust and relationship.

The Tithe Unlocks Supernatural Protection

Malachi 3:11 says:

"And I will rebuke the devourer for your sakes, so that he will not destroy the fruit of your ground."

- Tithing places a supernatural shield over our finances.
- God Himself rebukes the enemy from touching what belongs to us.
- When we tithe, we are not just blessed—we are protected.

Tithing Breaks the Spirit of Mammon

Matthew 6:24:

"No one can serve two masters; for either he will hate the one and love the other, or else he will be loyal to the one and despise the other. You cannot serve God and mammon."

- Tithing declares that God—not money—is our master.
- It shifts our dependence from finances to faith.

- When we tithe, we break fear and step into Kingdom abundance.

Biblical Examples of Tithing and Covenant Blessing

- Abraham tithed before the law (Genesis 14:20) and was called the father of faith.
- Jacob vowed to tithe (Genesis 28:22), and God prospered him abundantly.
- Jesus affirmed tithing (Matthew 23:23), showing it is still a Kingdom principle.

The Tithe Connects Us to God's Economy

- Tithing is not a bill—it's a spiritual investment.
- When we tithe, we activate the blessing and protection of God.
- Tithing is a divine connection to provision, overflow, and supernatural increase!

PowerPoint:

Tithing isn't about giving—it's about covenant! When we honor God first, He opens the windows of heaven over our lives!

42.

Divine Provision Is Attached to Obedience

Scripture: 1 Kings 17:13-14

"And Elijah said to her, 'Do not fear; go and do as you have said, but make me a small cake from it first, and bring it to me; and afterward make some for yourself and your son. For thus says the Lord God of Israel: "The bin of flour shall not be used up, nor shall the jar of oil run dry, until the day the Lord sends rain on the earth."'"

Obedience Activates God's Supply

Many people wait for **provision before they obey,** but in the Kingdom, obedience always comes first. The widow at Zarephath was facing a drought, limited resources, and fear, but when she obeyed the prophet's instruction, her miracle was released.

- She obeyed before she saw the provision.
- Her act of faith positioned her for supernatural supply.
- God's provision is often waiting on the other side of our obedience.

Faith Requires Action

James 2:17 tells us:

"Thus also faith by itself, if it does not have works, is dead."

- Obedience in giving is an act of faith that activates God's supernatural provision.
- If we wait to give until we "have enough," we may never step into abundance.
- Provision follows obedience, not the other way around!

God's Supply Is Always More Than Enough

- The widow expected **her last meal**—but God provided an endless supply.
- Peter obeyed Jesus and cast his net—he didn't just catch fish, his net **began to break from the overflow (Luke 5:4-6).**
- The disciples handed Jesus a small portion of bread and fish—**and He multiplied it to feed thousands (Matthew 14:17-20).**

When We Give in Obedience, God Responds with Overflow

Many believers struggle financially because they want to see before they sow. But God's pattern has always been:

1. Obey first.

2. Trust His Word.

3. Watch Him release supernatural provision!

God's Promise to the Obedient

Isaiah 1:19:

"If you are willing and obedient, you shall eat the good of the land."

- Obedience is the key to living in God's provision.
- When we bring the tithe, give offerings, and sow in faith, God ensures that we never lack.
- Divine supply is never limited by earthly circumstances!

PowerPoint:

Provision follows obedience! When we give in faith, we position ourselves for God's supernatural supply!

43.

God Is Looking for Stewards, Not Owners

Scripture: Psalm 24:1

"The earth is the Lord's, and all its fullness,
the world and those who dwell therein."

We Own Nothing—We Manage Everything

One of the greatest shifts we must make as believers is recognizing that **we are not owners—we are stewards.** Everything we have—our finances, our resources, our time—belongs to God.

- God owns it all, but He entrusts us with resources.
- We are managers, not masters.
- The way we handle what He gives us determines how much more He can trust us with.

Stewardship Is a Kingdom Responsibility

Jesus emphasized this in Luke 16:10:

"He who is faithful in what is least is faithful also in much; and he who is unjust in what is least is unjust also in much."

- If we handle what we have with wisdom and generosity, God will entrust us with more.

- If we are careless or selfish, we limit what He can place in our hands.
- Faithfulness in little leads to increase in much.

Breaking the Ownership Mentality

The world teaches us to **accumulate, hold on, and protect what we have**, but Kingdom thinking says:

- What we release, God multiplies.
- What we manage well, God increases.
- What we give, God replenishes abundantly.

Stewardship Is a Trust Test

Jesus said in Matthew 25:21:

"Well done, good and faithful servant; you were faithful over a few things, I will make you ruler over many things. Enter into the joy of your Lord."

- We are accountable for how we use what God places in our hands.
- We don't just steward money—we steward time, influence, and opportunities.
- If we prove faithful, God expands our capacity for greater Kingdom impact.

Living with an Open Hand

A steward knows:

Everything belongs to God.

We are conduits for His blessing, not hoarders of wealth.

God's provision flows through those He can trust.

PowerPoint:

We are not owners—we are stewards! When we handle what God gives us wisely, He entrusts us with more!

44.

Multiplication Is a Kingdom Principle

Scripture: 2 Kings 4:2, 6-7

"So Elisha said to her, 'What shall I do for you?
Tell me, what do you have in the house?'
And she said, 'Your maidservant has nothing
in the house but a jar of oil.' Then he said,
'Go, borrow vessels from everywhere, from all your
neighbors—empty vessels; do not gather just a few.'"

"And it came to pass, when the vessels were full,
that she said to her son, 'Bring me another vessel.'
And he said to her, 'There is not another vessel.'
So the oil ceased. Then she came and told the man
of God. And he said, 'Go, sell the oil and pay your debt;
and you and your sons live on the rest.'"

God Uses What We Surrender

The widow in 2 Kings 4 was in financial crisis. She had no way to pay her debts, and creditors were coming to take her sons as slaves. She cried out to the prophet Elisha, and his response was not to give her something new—it was to use **what she already had.**

- God asked, "What do you have?" because multiplication begins with what we already possess.
- She saw only a small jar of oil, but God saw potential for overflow.
- The moment she released what she had, God multiplied it.

Multiplication Requires an Act of Faith

Elisha instructed her to gather as many empty vessels as possible. The number of vessels determined the size of her miracle.

- Had she gathered only a few, she would have received a small blessing.
- Because she gathered many, the oil kept flowing until every vessel was full!
- The multiplication stopped only when she ran out of capacity to receive!

Giving Creates Space for Increase

- Many people wait for more before they give—but multiplication happens when we step out in faith.
- What we hold on to stays the same, but what we release to God is multiplied.
- When we create space for God to work, He fills it!

We Sow, God Multiplies

Paul reinforces this in 2 Corinthians 9:10:

"Now may He who supplies seed to the sower, and bread for food, supply and multiply the seed you have sown and increase the fruits of your righteousness."

- God provides the seed, but it must be sown to be multiplied.
- What we give in faith, He expands beyond what we could ever expect.
- The measure of our faith determines the measure of our increase.

Multiplication Is God's Response to Faith

- If the widow had limited her faith, then she would have limited her miracle.
- When we give, we don't lose—we make room for God's abundance.
- God's Kingdom is built on multiplication, not subtraction!

PowerPoint:

What we give, God multiplies! The size of our faith determines the size of our increase!

45.

Seed Produces After Its Kind

Scripture: Galatians 6:7

"Do not be deceived, God is not mocked;
for whatever a man sows, that he will also reap."

The Law of Reproduction in the Kingdom

One of the foundational laws God established in creation is that **everything produces after its own kind.** We see this in nature:

- Apple seeds produce apple trees.
- Wheat seeds produce wheat fields.
- Corn seeds don't produce oranges—each seed multiplies according to what was sown.

Paul tells us in Galatians that **this principle applies spiritually and financially as well—what we sow, we will reap!**

You Reap What You Sow

Some people wonder why they aren't seeing a harvest in their lives, but the question isn't why hasn't God blessed me? The real question is: What have I sown?

- If I sow love, I will reap love.
- If I sow generosity, then I will reap generosity.

- If I sow financial seed, I will reap financial increase.
- If I don't sow anything, I can't expect a harvest!

Sowing Determines the Harvest

2 Corinthians 9:6 says:

"He who sows sparingly will also reap sparingly, and he who sows bountifully will also reap bountifully."

- We decide the size of our harvest by the size of our seed.
- The more we release, the greater our return.
- A farmer who plants a small handful of seeds can't expect a massive harvest—he reaps according to what he has sown!

Don't Just Pray for a Harvest—Plant for a Harvest

Many people pray for financial blessing but never take the step of sowing. But we cannot reap what we have not planted.

- Prayer doesn't replace planting—it prepares us to plant.
- God multiplies what we sow, not what we wish for.
- If we sow in faith, we can expect a supernatural return!

What Are You Sowing Today?

- If you need financial increase, sow financial seed.

- If you need breakthrough, sow into someone else's breakthrough.
- If you need favor, be a blessing to others.

PowerPoint:

Seed produces after its own kind! If we want to reap a harvest, we must be intentional about what we sow!

46.

Giving with Expectation

Scripture: Mark 11:24

"Therefore I say to you, whatever things you ask when you pray, believe that you receive them, and you will have them."

Faith-Filled Giving Produces a Harvest

Many believers give out of **obedience**, which is good, but few give with **expectation**—believing for a supernatural return. Yet Jesus Himself teaches that when we give, we should expect a return.

- Expectation is not greed—it is faith.
- Sowing without expectation is like planting a seed but never looking for the harvest.
- Faith is the bridge between sowing and reaping!

Biblical Examples of Expectant Giving

1. Abraham—Expecting a Generational Harvest

Genesis 22:16-17:

"By Myself I have sworn," says the Lord, because you have done this thing, and have not withheld your son, your only son—blessing I will bless you, and multiplying I will multiply your descendants as the stars of the heaven and

as the sand which is on the seashore; and your descendants shall possess the gate of their enemies."

- Abraham gave his most valuable possession—his son Isaac—in faith, believing God would provide.
- God responded by not only returning Isaac but also blessing Abraham with a generational covenant of prosperity and dominion.
- When we give in faith, we are not just expecting for today—we are sowing into generations!

2. The Widow at Zarephath—Expecting Divine Provision

1 Kings 17:13-14:

"Elijah said to her, 'Do not fear; go and do as you have said, but make me a small cake from it first, and bring it to me; and afterward make some for yourself and your son. For thus says the Lord God of Israel: "The bin of flour shall not be used up, nor shall the jar of oil run dry, until the day the Lord sends rain on the earth."""

- This widow was preparing for lack, but when she gave in obedience, she received supernatural supply.
- She expected to eat her last meal, but God gave her a continuous flow of provision.
- God doesn't just meet needs—He sustains us when we expect Him to move!

3. Peter's Boat—Expecting Overflow

Luke 5:4-6:

"When He had stopped speaking, He said to Simon, 'Launch out into the deep and let down your nets for a catch.' But Simon answered and said to Him, 'Master, we have toiled all night and caught nothing; nevertheless at Your word I will let down the net.' And when they had done this, they caught a great number of fish, and their net was breaking."

- Peter had been fishing all night with no success, but at Jesus's word, he cast his net in faith.
- Not only did he receive a catch, but also it was more than he could handle—his boat began to sink from the overflow!
- God always responds to obedience with more than enough!

Why Some People Don't See a Return

Some believers give but never expect anything in return—not realizing that faith is required. Giving without faith is like planting a seed without watering it!

- Expectation activates the harvest.
- If we don't believe for a return, then we may not recognize it when it comes.
- God is a rewarder, and faith-filled givers position themselves to receive.

Faith and Generosity Work Together

Luke 6:38:

"Give, and it will be given to you: good measure, pressed down, shaken together, and running over will be put into your bosom."

- Jesus Himself connects giving with receiving!
- God designed generosity to produce increase—not just for us, but so we can bless others.
- We give in faith, and we expect in faith!

Expectancy Is a Kingdom Mindset

- We expect natural seeds to grow—so why wouldn't we expect spiritual seeds to produce?
- God loves a cheerful giver, but He also honors a faith-filled giver.
- When we give, we should be looking for supernatural opportunities, open doors, and divine favor.

PowerPoint:

Giving without expectation is like planting a seed but never looking for the harvest. Expect God to move when you give!

47.

God's Blessing Is Generational

Scripture: Psalm 112:1-3

"Blessed is the man who fears the Lord, who delights greatly in His commandments. His descendants will be mighty on earth; the generation of the upright will be blessed. Wealth and riches will be in his house, and his righteousness endures forever."

The Blessing of God Is Meant to Outlive You

One of the biggest misconceptions about financial blessing is that it's only about personal provision—but the Bible makes it clear that God's blessing is generational. What He does in your life isn't just meant to provide for just today—it's meant to set up future generations for success.

- We don't serve a "just enough" God—we serve the God of "more than enough."
- A Kingdom-minded giver doesn't just think about today's needs—they think about legacy.
- What we do with our resources today will impact generations to come!

God is looking for people He can trust with resources not just to bless them, but to establish His covenant through them for generations.

Biblical Examples of Generational Blessing

1. Abraham: A Legacy of Faith and Wealth

Genesis 12:2-3:

"I will make you a great nation; I will bless you and make your name great; and you shall be a blessing ... And in you all the families of the earth shall be blessed."

- God's blessing over Abraham wasn't just for him—it was for generations after him.
- Isaac, Jacob, and the entire nation of Israel walked in the overflow of what Abraham established.
- Abraham tithed, and his descendants reaped the benefits of his faithfulness.

2. David and Solomon: Generational Wealth and Wisdom

1 Kings 3:12-13:

"Behold, I have done according to your words; see, I have given you a wise and understanding heart... And I have also given you what you have not asked: both riches and honor."

- David had a heart after God, and Solomon inherited both his wisdom and wealth.

- Solomon built the temple using the resources David had set aside—what David started, Solomon completed.
- When we store up resources and faithfulness today, our children and grandchildren will walk in it.

What You Pass Down Matters

Every family has something they pass down—it might be a poverty mindset, a lack mentality, or a spirit of fear about money. But in the Kingdom, we have the opportunity to pass down faith, financial blessing, and supernatural provision!

- We can break generational cycles of poverty through faith-filled giving.
- Our children should see us trusting God, giving generously, and walking in supernatural supply.
- What you model today will be multiplied in your children's lives tomorrow.

How to Position Your Family for Generational Blessing

1. **Teach Stewardship Early** – Teach your children and spiritual sons and daughters that everything belongs to God, and we are just managers (Psalm 24:1).
2. **Break Poverty Thinking** – Reject small thinking and teach faith-filled generosity. Kingdom

people don't think in scarcity—they think in abundance.

3. **Tithe and Give Generously** – Show your family that giving is part of trusting God. It's not about "losing money"—it's about stewarding and multiplying resources.
4. **Build for the Next Generation** – Make financial decisions today that will leave a spiritual and financial inheritance for your children and grandchildren.

Generosity Creates Generational Favor

- When we obey God with our finances, the favor that follows impacts future generations.
- God desires to bless His people so that their children will never experience lack.
- What we release in faith today will continue producing long after we're gone.

Proverbs 13:22 says:

"A good man leaves an inheritance to his children's children, but the wealth of the sinner is stored up for the righteous."

- We are not just called to survive—we are called to build, expand, and leave a legacy.
- Our giving today isn't just about us—it's about making sure the next generation walks in the fullness of God's blessing!

Breaking the Generational Curse of Lack

Many believers struggle financially not because God hasn't provided, but because they have inherited a mindset of lack.

- "Money is evil." ➞ No, the love of money is evil. (1 Timothy 6:10)
- "We will never have enough." ➞ No, God supplies all our needs. (Philippians 4:19)
- "Rich people are greedy." ➞ No, God wants us to prosper to build His Kingdom. (3 John 2)

Just as we can pass down faith, we can also pass down fear, doubt, and financial bondage. It's time to break the cycle!

You Are the Turning Point for Your Family

- Your faithfulness will create opportunities your children and grandchildren won't have to fight for.
- Your obedience in giving will unlock doors of favor for future generations.
- You are shifting your family line from financial struggle to Kingdom prosperity!

Psalm 37:25:

"I have been young, and now am old; yet I have not seen the righteous forsaken, nor his descendants begging bread."

- God's promise is that those who walk uprightly will see their descendants walk in supernatural supply.
- Your faithfulness today secures tomorrow's overflow!

PowerPoint:

What we give today doesn't just bless us—it creates a legacy of blessing for generations!

48.

Giving Breaks the Spirit of Lack

Scripture: 2 Kings 4:42-44

"Then a man came from Baal Shalisha, and brought the man of God bread of the firstfruits, twenty loaves of barley bread, and newly ripened grain in his knapsack. And he said, 'Give it to the people, that they may eat.' But his servant said, 'What? Shall I set this before one hundred men?' He said again, 'Give it to the people, that they may eat; for thus says the Lord: "They shall eat and have some left over."' So he set it before them; and they ate and had some left over, according to the word of the Lord."

The Spirit of Lack vs. The Spirit of Faith

Many people struggle with the **fear of not having enough**—this is what we call the spirit of lack. It is a mindset that says:

- "I don't have enough to give."
- "If I give, I might not be able to pay my bills."
- "I need to hold on to what I have just in case."

But God's economy doesn't operate on scarcity—it operates on faith!

- The world says, "Hold on to what you have."

- The Kingdom says, "Release what's in your hand, and God will multiply it."

The servant in 2 Kings 4 had a **lack mentality**—he couldn't see how twenty loaves could feed a hundred men. But Elisha had faith in God's provision, and as a result, there was more than enough!

Lack Is Not Just a Financial Condition—It's a Spiritual Condition

Lack isn't just about **having no money**—it's about how we **think about money.**

- A person with a lack mentality could have $100,000 in the bank and still feel broke.
- A person with a Kingdom mindset could have very little but walk in peace and faith.
- Lack says, "There's never enough."
- Faith says, "God is more than enough!"

Giving breaks the grip of lack because it forces us to trust God as our provider instead of trusting in money.

The Widow at Zarephath: Breaking the Fear of Lack

1 Kings 17:12-16

"So she said, 'As the Lord your God lives, I do not have bread, only a handful of flour in a bin, and a little oil in a jar...'"

- The widow thought she was preparing her last meal.
- She believed there was no future provision.
- She was operating in a spirit of lack!

But when she obeyed the word of the Lord through Elijah and gave first, the oil and flour never ran out.

- The moment she shifted from fear to faith, she stepped into supernatural supply.
- She moved from lack to overflow.
- Giving positioned her for a miracle!

Giving Moves You from Survival to Supernatural Supply

Many people **stay stuck in survival mode** because they never **activate** the law of giving and receiving.

- They pray for provision but refuse to sow.
- They want a harvest but won't plant a seed.
- They expect God to increase what they aren't willing to release.

Galatians 6:7 says:

"Do not be deceived, God is not mocked; for whatever a man sows, that he will also reap."

- The only way to reap is to sow.
- The only way to see increase is to step out in faith.
- If you want to break lack, you have to give in faith!

Jesus and the Feeding of the 5,000

Jesus demonstrated this Kingdom principle when He fed the 5,000:

- The disciples focused on what they DIDN'T have.
- Jesus focused on what they were willing to release.
- The miracle didn't happen in their hands—it happened in Jesus's hands!

Matthew 14:19-20

"Then He took the five loaves and the two fish, and looking up to heaven, He blessed and broke and gave the loaves to the disciples... So they all ate and were filled, and they took up twelve baskets full of the fragments that remained."

- If the boy had held on to his lunch, he would have stayed in lack.
- Because he gave, there was more than enough!
- God is always ready to multiply, but He needs us to trust Him enough to release what we have!

How to Break the Spirit of Lack in Your Life

Renew Your Mindset About Money – Lack is a mindset before it's a financial condition. If you believe God is your provider, then you will walk in His provision!

Trust God's Word Over Your Bank Account – Faith is not based on what you see—it's based on what God has spoken!

Sow Even When It Feels Uncomfortable – Giving in a difficult season is how you activate supernatural supply.

Stop Saying "I Can't Afford to Give" – That's a lie from the enemy! You can't afford NOT to give!

Expect God to Multiply What You Release – The miracle is in the release! If you release it in faith, God will bring the increase.

A Testimony of Breaking Lack

There are countless testimonies of people I have encountered at church and other places who have stepped out in faith through giving and have seen God provide supernaturally.

- **One businessman** was struggling financially but decided to give sacrificially into his church. Within weeks, new business contracts opened up, and his income tripled.
- **A single mother** felt led to tithe even when her finances were tight—shortly after, she received unexpected provision through a new job opportunity and supernatural favor.
- **A church that was behind on their mortgage** decided to sow into missions—and within months,

they received a large donation that cleared their debt!

Why? Because giving activates the law of supernatural supply!

God's Promise to Those Who Give in Faith

Malachi 3:10

"Bring all the tithes into the storehouse, that there may be food in My house, and try Me now in this," says the Lord of hosts, "If I will not open for you the windows of heaven and pour out for you such blessing that there will not be room enough to receive it."

- When we trust God with our giving, He responds with supernatural provision.
- When we release what's in our hands, God releases what's in His.
- We don't give to get—we give to honor God, and increase is a byproduct!

Final Thought: Giving Is a War Against the Spirit of Lack

When you give, you are making a **bold declaration:**

"I am not limited by what I see—I am governed by God's supernatural economy!"

"I refuse to let fear dictate my giving—I give by faith, and I expect increase!"

"Lack has no power over me—I walk in Kingdom overflow!

PowerPoint:

Giving isn't just generosity—it's warfare against the spirit of lack. When we give, we declare that God is our limitless provider!

49.

The Flow of Generosity Brings Supernatural Favor

Scripture: Proverbs 3:9-10

"Honor the Lord with your possessions, and with the firstfruits of all your increase; so your barns will be filled with plenty, and your vats will overflow with new wine."

Generosity Opens the Door for God's Favor

There is a direct connection between generosity and supernatural favor. When we choose to honor God with what we have, He responds by opening the windows of heaven over our lives.

- Generosity isn't just about finances—it's a posture of the heart.
- When we live with an open hand, God fills it with more than enough.
- Giving doesn't just impact our financial life—it releases favor in every area!

Many people think giving is about subtraction, but in the Kingdom, giving multiplies what we have. It places us in a position to receive from the unlimited resources of heaven!

Giving Is a Key to Open Heaven

The Bible is filled with examples of how giving activates favor and increase.

1. The Favor of the Firstfruits (Proverbs 3:9-10)

God doesn't just ask us to give randomly—He asks us to honor Him first.

- The firstfruits principle is about putting God first in every area, including finances.
- God promises that when we honor Him first, our barns will be filled with plenty.
- Overflow is the result of a lifestyle of honor and generosity!

2. The Widow in Zarephath (1 Kings 17:12-16)

- She was in lack but chose to give first to Elijah.
- Because she honored God with what she had, supernatural favor rested on her home.
- Her flour and oil never ran out!

3. The Philippian Church (Philippians 4:15-19)

- They were generous in supporting Paul's ministry.
- As a result, Paul declared that "God shall supply all your need according to His riches in glory."
- Their generosity unlocked supernatural provision!

Generosity and Favor Go Hand in Hand

Many people pray for favor but never activate it through generosity.

- Favor follows those who are faithful stewards.
- When we give, we position ourselves under an open heaven.
- God's favor brings opportunities, divine connections, and supernatural provision.

Luke 6:38:

"Give, and it will be given to you: good measure, pressed down, shaken together, and running over will be put into your bosom."

- When we give, God doesn't just return the same amount—He multiplies it!
- "Running over" means God gives us more than we expect.
- Favor is when God opens doors no man can shut.

What Happens When We Live Generously?

We Step into Overflow

- God's economy is not limited by the world's economy.
- When we give, we tap into supernatural supply.
- The more we pour out, the more God pours in.

We Walk in Divine Connections

- Generosity creates favor with both God and man.
- Many promotions, opportunities, and breakthroughs happen because of giving.

- Favor isn't just financial—it's relational, spiritual, and practical.

We Break the Cycle of Lack

- When we withhold, we stay in lack.
- When we give, we move into abundance.
- Giving declares that we trust God as our provider!

A Lifestyle of Generosity Produces a Lifestyle of Favor

The favor of God is not random—it follows those who walk in obedience and trust.

Psalm 5:12:

"For You, O Lord, will bless the righteous; with favor You will surround him as with a shield."

- God's favor surrounds those who honor Him with their resources.
- A lifestyle of generosity brings continuous supernatural increase.
- If we want to live in God's favor, we must live with an open hand.

Generosity Sets the Course for Supernatural Favor

Giving is more than a financial decision—it is a supernatural key that unlocks blessing, favor, and increase.

"Giving isn't just about money—it's about positioning yourself under God's supernatural flow of favor!"

"Generosity isn't a loss—it's the seed for your next breakthrough!"

"When we honor God first, He ensures that we never lack!"

PowerPoint:

When we honor God with our resources, we step into supernatural favor, open doors, and divine increase!

50.

The Test of Prosperity

Scripture: Deuteronomy 8:11-14

"Beware that you do not forget the Lord your God by not keeping His commandments, His judgments, and His statutes which I command you today, lest—when you have eaten and are full, and have built beautiful houses and dwell in them; and when your herds and your flocks multiply, and your silver and your gold are multiplied, and all that you have is multiplied; when your heart is lifted up, and you forget the Lord your God..."

The Greater Test: Poverty or Prosperity?

Most people believe lack is the greatest test of faith, but the Bible warns that prosperity can be an even greater test!

- When people struggle financially, they depend on God for provision.
- But when people experience abundance, they are tempted to forget the One who blessed them.
- Money doesn't change people—it reveals what's already in their hearts.

Staying Humble in Abundance

The Bible is full of examples of people who failed the test of prosperity:

- Solomon started with wisdom but allowed wealth to lead him into compromise (1 Kings 11:1-4).
- The rich fool in Jesus's parable stored up wealth for himself but didn't invest in the Kingdom (Luke 12:16-21).
- Israel prospered under God's blessing but constantly turned away when things were "good" (Deuteronomy 32:15).

How to Pass the Test of Prosperity

1. Stay dependent on God, no matter how much He blesses you.
2. Keep generosity at the center of your financial life.
3. Always remember that wealth is a tool for Kingdom impact, not personal comfort.

Abundance Should Make Us More Generous, Not More Selfish

- If wealth makes us give less, we are failing the test.
- If success makes us less prayerful, we are missing the point.
- The more God gives, the more we should pour out!

PowerPoint:

Abundance is a test—will you stay surrendered to God as He blesses you?

51.

Obedience: The Key to Your Breakthrough

Scripture: Isaiah 1:19

"If you are willing and obedient,
you shall eat the good of the land."

Breakthrough Follows Obedience

Many people pray for financial breakthrough, but they struggle to obey the principles that unlock it. God's blessings are not random—they follow obedience to His Word and His ways.

- Faith and obedience go hand in hand.
- You cannot ask for God's provision while refusing to follow His instructions.
- Breakthrough in finances doesn't come from wishful thinking—it comes from faith-filled action.

When we obey God, we position ourselves to receive the fullness of His provision. The key to financial breakthrough is not waiting on God—it's aligning our actions with His principles.

Biblical Examples of Financial Breakthrough Through Obedience

1. Peter's Fishing Business (Luke 5:4-7)

"When He had stopped speaking, He said to Simon, 'Launch out into the deep and let down your nets for a catch.' But Simon answered and said to Him, 'Master, we have toiled all night and caught nothing; nevertheless, at Your word I will let down the net.' And when they had done this, they caught a great number of fish, and their net was breaking."

- Peter had already worked all night and caught nothing.
- Logic said it was pointless—but obedience said, "Do it anyway."
- The moment Peter obeyed Jesus, his financial situation changed.
- His boat went from empty to overflowing simply because he followed an instruction.

2. The Widow's Oil (2 Kings 4:1-7)

- The widow was in debt and about to lose her sons to slavery.
- Elisha gave her a divine instruction: Gather as many jars as possible and pour the little oil she had into them.
- As long as she obeyed, the oil kept flowing!

- Her breakthrough wasn't just in prayer—it was in her response to the instruction given.

What Happens When We Obey?

1. Obedience Opens the Door for Provision

- Many people ask God to bless them, but they don't follow the steps He's given in His Word.
- Tithing, sowing, generosity, and wise stewardship all align us with God's financial system.

2. Obedience Activates Favor

- Joseph's obedience in managing Egypt's resources positioned him for favor and promotion.
- Financial breakthrough often comes through divine opportunities that are unlocked by obedience.

3. Obedience Breaks the Spirit of Lack

- Fear says, "I can't afford to give." Faith says, "I can't afford not to obey."
- When we obey God, we step out of fear and into the flow of supernatural provision.

Delayed Obedience Is Still Disobedience

Many times, people say, "I'll obey when my situation improves." But delayed obedience is still disobedience.

- Tithing when you "can afford it" is not faith—it's convenience.

- Sowing "when things get better" means you're still trusting circumstances, not God.
- Obedience must be immediate if we want to see God move in our finances.

How to Walk in Financial Obedience

1. Obey in the Small Things First

- Faithfulness in little leads to greater increase (Luke 16:10).
- Start tithing, giving, and managing your finances according to Kingdom principles.

2. Follow God's Instructions Even When They Don't Make Sense

- Peter didn't see results until he obeyed (Luke 5:4-7).
- Financial obedience often challenges human reasoning, but faith acts on God's Word, not on what makes sense.

3. Trust God's Timing in Your Obedience

- God honors faith-filled, consistent obedience, not just occasional giving.
- The breakthrough may not always be immediate, but when you obey, God is faithful to His promises.

PowerPoint:

"Financial breakthrough isn't random—it follows obedience to God's principles!"

52.

The Connection Between Worship and Giving

Scripture: Matthew 2:11

"And when they had come into the house, they saw the young Child with Mary His mother, and fell down and worshiped Him. And when they had opened their treasures, they presented gifts to Him: gold, frankincense, and myrrh."

Giving Is an Act of Worship

Many people separate their giving from their worship, but in the Bible, worship and giving are always connected.

- True worship is not just lifting our hands—it's laying down what we value.
- Giving is a response to God's presence.
- If worship doesn't cost us something, is it really worship?

When the wise men visited Jesus, they did not come empty-handed—they brought gifts as part of their worship.

- They gave treasures, not leftovers.

- They recognized Jesus as King and honored Him with valuable gifts.
- Our giving should reflect the value we place on God in our lives.

Biblical Examples of Giving as Worship

1. Abraham: Worship Through Sacrifice (Genesis 22:2-5)

"Stay here with the donkey; the lad and I will go yonder and worship, and we will come back to you."

- God tested Abraham's faith by asking for what was most valuable—his son, Isaac.
- Abraham called this a form of "worship" before even knowing how God would provide.
- God provided a ram, showing that when we give in faith, God responds with provision.

2. David: "I Will Not Give That Which Costs Me Nothing" (2 Samuel 24:24)

"Then the king said to Araunah, 'No, but I will surely buy it from you for a price; nor will I offer burnt offerings to the Lord my God with that which costs me nothing.'"

- David understood that true worship requires sacrifice.
- He refused to give an offering that had no personal value.

- When we give, it should be from a place of faith, honor, and personal cost.

3. The Poor Widow: Worship Through Sacrificial Giving (Mark 12:42-44)

"So He called His disciples to Himself and said to them, 'Assuredly, I say to you that this poor widow has put in more than all those who have given to the treasury ... but she out of her poverty put in all that she had, her whole livelihood.'"

- The widow gave out of faith, not excess.
- Jesus measured her giving by the level of sacrifice, not the amount of money.
- Giving is not about what we have—it's about the heart behind it.

The Connection Between Worship and Firstfruits

Proverbs 3:9-10 says:

"Honor the Lord with your possessions, and with the firstfruits of all your increase; so your barns will be filled with plenty, and your vats will overflow with new wine."

- The principle of "firstfruits" is about giving to God first, not last.
- When we give our first and best, we acknowledge that He is our provider.
- Firstfruits giving is an act of trust and worship, positioning us for overflow.

Why Worship and Giving Are Connected

- Worship is about placing God first. Giving is about placing God first in our finances.
- Worship is an act of surrender. Giving requires surrender and faith.
- Worship acknowledges God as King. Giving honors Him as the source of all we have.

Giving is never just a financial transaction—it is a spiritual act of worship that aligns our heart with God's.

PowerPoint:

Giving is not just generosity—it is worship! When we give, we acknowledge God as our source and King!

BONUS:

Divine Strategies for Increase

Scripture: Isaiah 48:17

"Thus says the Lord, your Redeemer, the Holy One of Israel: 'I am the Lord your God, who teaches you to profit, who leads you by the way you should go.'"

God Provides More Than Money—He Provides Strategies

Many people pray for financial breakthrough but don't realize that God's primary way of bringing increase isn't just dropping money from heaven—it's giving divine wisdom and strategies.

- God doesn't just provide for us—He teaches us how to create and manage wealth.
- If we want financial increase, we must seek not just provision, but revelation.
- Miracles happen, but more often, financial breakthrough comes through divine ideas, opportunities, and strategies.

Psalm 37:23 says:

"The steps of a good man are ordered by the Lord, and He delights in his way."

- God orders our steps toward increase, but we must be willing to follow.
- Many miss their breakthrough because they're waiting for money instead of seeking God's direction.

Biblical Examples of Financial Strategies Given by God

1. Joseph: A Strategy for Economic Expansion (Genesis 41:33-36)

Joseph didn't pray just for God to provide food during famine—he received a divine strategy to manage Egypt's economy.

- Through God-given wisdom, he stored grain during years of abundance.
- When famine hit, Egypt became the wealthiest nation because it was prepared.
- Financial wisdom comes through revelation, planning, and stewardship.

2. Jacob: A Supernatural Business Plan (Genesis 30:37-43)

Jacob worked for Laban and had no wealth of his own—but through divine instruction, he gained supernatural increase.

- God gave Jacob insight on how to multiply livestock.

- His obedience to God's strategy resulted in exponential increase.
- God has creative solutions for every financial situation!

3. Peter: A Supernatural Business Instruction (Luke 5:4-7)

Peter fished all night with no success—but Jesus gave him a divine instruction:

"Launch out into the deep and let down your nets for a catch."

- Peter's breakthrough didn't come from working harder—it came from obeying God's word.
- Financial increase often comes from simple acts of obedience to divine strategy.
- Peter went from empty to overflowing nets because he followed God's direction.

How to Access Divine Financial Strategies

1. Seek God's Wisdom Daily

- James 1:5: *"If any of you lacks wisdom, let him ask of God, who gives to all liberally and without reproach, and it will be given to him."*
- Pray not just for money, but for God's wisdom to steward what He provides.

2. Be Open to Unconventional Solutions

- Sometimes, God's strategy won't make sense in the natural world.

- The widow in 2 Kings 4 was told to borrow empty jars—her miracle required action!
- Don't limit God to traditional methods—He often works through creative opportunities.

3. Act on What God Reveals

- Revelation without action is wasted.
- Peter's nets filled only when he cast them into the water.
- Many people have ideas from God but never act on them—faith requires movement!

4. Be Faithful with What You Have

- Luke 16:10: *"He who is faithful in what is least is faithful also in much."*
- If you manage little well, God will entrust you with more.

5. Align Your Finances with Kingdom Priorities

- Matthew 6:33: *"Seek first the Kingdom of God and His righteousness, and all these things shall be added to you."*
- God's strategies come when we put Him first—when we handle finances with Kingdom purpose, He ensures we walk in provision.

Why Some People Never Experience Financial Breakthrough

Many people pray for increase but never see it because they fail to recognize the strategies God is giving them.

- They expect a financial miracle but ignore divine opportunities.
- They resist stepping out in faith when God gives an instruction.
- They continue old habits instead of seeking God's wisdom for new strategies.

Breaking Through Financial Stagnation

If you feel stuck financially, then ask yourself:

- Have I been faithful with what God has already given me?
- Am I ignoring divine strategies because they don't look the way I expected?
- Am I waiting for provision when God is waiting for obedience?

PowerPoint:

"God doesn't just provide—He gives wisdom, ideas, and strategies to multiply what He puts in your hands!"

ABOUT THE AUTHOR

Ron Eivaz is the senior pastor of Harvest Church, a vibrant, multi-campus church based in Turlock, California, known for revival, discipleship, and advancing the Kingdom of God. With over thirty years of ministry experience, Ron leads with a strong apostolic voice and a deep passion for revival, the move of the Holy Spirit, and building healthy, effective leaders.

He holds degrees from Oral Roberts University and Regent University and is widely respected for mentoring leaders in both ministry and government spheres. Ron is the founder of the Harvest Ministry Network—a growing community of churches and leaders committed to revival, healthy leadership, and long-term Kingdom impact. He also co-hosts the *Harvest Ministry Network Leadership Podcast,* which he equips pastors and leaders to walk in faith, lead with integrity, and multiply Kingdom influence.

Ron and his wife, Jennifer, continue to serve the Church with conviction and compassion, committed to seeing lives and communities transformed by the presence and power of God.

STAY CONNECTED WITH RON EIVAZ

Thanks for reading *Kingdom Multiplication*. If this book encouraged or challenged you, I'd love to stay connected and help you take the next step.

Online & Resources

Website: www.roneivaz.com

Church: www.harvestonline.church

Podcast: *Harvest Ministry Network Leadership Podcast*

Follow on Social Media

Instagram: @roneivaz

Facebook: @facebook.com/ron.eivaz

YouTube: youtube.com/@Harvestonline.church